495

Galley

MENUS AROUND THE WORLD

MAYFLOWER BOOKS, INC., U.S.A.
575 Lexington Avenue
New York, New York 10022

CONTENTS

Around the world
　In smart cuisines
Fragrant dishes
　Steal the scenes.

To tempt the taste
　Or catch the eye...
A potpourri of
　Foods to try.

Regal treats or
　Humble fare...
Recipes from
　Everywhere!

A festive dish,
　A special treat,
That perfect touch!
　Bon Appetit!

Alice Leedy Mason

*Various meat pictures co
National Live Stock & Meat*

Australia occupies an entire continent, and its cuisine is much like that of England, with beef, fish and fruit greatly favored.

EGG-TOPPED BURGERS

3 T. butter or margarine
2 T. water
1 lb. ground beef, chuck or round
1 T. salt
¼ t. pepper
2 English muffins, halved and toasted
4 fried eggs
   Paprika
   Onion slices

In a large saucepan, sauté onions in the butter until brown. Add water and cover. Simmer until tender. Mix beef with salt and pepper. Shape into 4 patties. In a large skillet fry hamburger patties over medium heat on each side until done. Place a patty on each muffin half. Top with onions and then with a fried egg. Sprinkle with paprika. Serve open face.

Kathy Mead

PUMPKIN SOUP

2 lbs. pumpkin, peeled	½ t. pepper
	1 T. flour
2 onions, chopped	¼ c. cold water
6 c. stock	1 c. light cream
1 t. salt	Chopped parsley

Cut pumpkin into ½-inch cubes, removing seeds and fiber. Place in a saucepan with the onions, stock and seasoning. Cook over low heat until pumpkin is soft, about 1 hour. Put pumpkin through a sieve or puree in electric blender. Return to saucepan. Combine flour and water and stir until smooth. Add to the soup, stirring constantly, until it begins to boil. Lastly, add the cream. Mix well. Garnish with chopped parsley.

TOAD-IN-THE-HOLE

1 lb. sausage meat	1 t. baking powder
1 c. flour	2 eggs
¼ t. salt	1 c. milk

Shape sausage into 1-inch balls and place in a 2-quart casserole. Bake 15 or 20 minutes until lightly browned. Pour off most of the fat from the casserole, leaving about ¼ cup. While sausage bakes, sift flour, baking powder and salt together in a bowl. Add milk and eggs. Mix together lightly and beat the mixture together well until very smooth. Pour into the hot casserole over the sausage balls and bake 15 minutes in a preheated 400° oven. Reduce oven heat to 350° and bake another 15 minutes. Serve immediately. Good with cool applesauce.

Mrs. J. Davidson

ABBREVIATIONS

t.—teaspoon
T.—tablespoon
c.—cup
pkg.—package
pt.—pint
qt.—quart
oz.—ounce
lb.—pound

FRUIT SALAD

1 medium pineapple, halved and
  quartered lengthwise
¼ c. orange juice
2 T. sugar
½ c. fresh strawberries
1 banana, sliced
1 c. preserved peaches
1 c. canned papaw
  Macadamia nuts or almonds
  Coconut

Remove pineapple from shell. Refrigerate the shells. Discard pineapple core. Cut pineapple into ½-inch wedges. In a large bowl combine orange juice and sugar. Mix well. Add fruit. Stir, then cover. Refrigerate at least 1 hour. To serve, mound fruit in pineapple shells. Sprinkle with nuts and coconut.

THREE-BEAN SALAD

3 10-oz. cans three-bean mix
¾ c. fresh sliced green beans, lightly
  cooked
¾ c. celery, sliced diagonally
1 small onion, thinly sliced
1 green pepper, finely chopped

Wash beans and drain. Combine all ingredients.

DRESSING

½ c. sugar
½ c. white vinegar (warmed to dissolve
  sugar)
½ c. salad oil
1 t. salt
½ t. pepper

Combine ingredients. Pour dressing over bean mixture. It will keep two months if placed in screw-top jars in the refrigerator.

Mrs. J. I. Grenfell

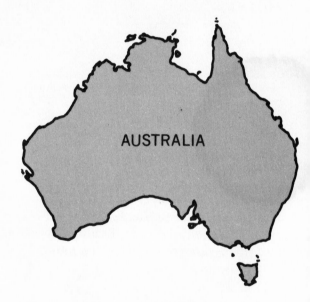

AUSTRALIA

PAVLOVA

3 egg whites	¾ t. sugar
¼ t. cream of tartar	1 t. vanilla

Preheat oven to 275°. Beat egg whites and cream of tartar until quite stiff; fold in sugar, then add vanilla. Place on greased paper on a greased baking sheet and bake 1½ to 2 hours at 275°. Do not open oven door during baking time. Turn oven off. Leave in oven with door closed, at least 1 hour. Remove from oven. Before serving pile with whipped cream and decorate with chopped fruit.

Margaret Carlson

AUSTRIA

PUSZTA SCHNITZEL

1½ lbs. veal steak, cut in 1-inch cubes
¼ c. flour
3 T. shortening, melted
2 T. minced onion
1 T. chopped parsley
½ t. salt
¼ t. paprika
¼ t. celery salt
1 c. soup stock
½ c. sour cream

Roll meat in the flour. Add the onion and veal to the melted shortening and brown well. Add parsley, salt, paprika, celery salt and stock. Simmer 1 hour. Add sour cream and heat well. Do not boil. Add to taste: chopped green pepper, sautéed sliced mushrooms, tomato wedges, diced boiled carrots. Heat. Serve with broad noodles. Serves 4.

Austria, land of snow-covered mountains, occupies a central location on the European continent. Food specialties include schnitzels, tortes and the most popular single dish, boiled beef.

SMOKED PORK PLATTER

1 boneless smoked pork shoulder roll (approximately 2½ lbs.)
  Water
4 medium potatoes, pared and halved
3 small onions, quartered
1 27-oz. can sauerkraut
1 t. caraway seed
¼ t. pepper (optional)

Place pork shoulder roll in a Dutch oven and add enough water to cover meat. Cover and cook over low heat 1 hour and 30 minutes. Remove meat from pan and pour off all but 2 cups of liquid. Add potatoes and onions to liquid in pan. Place meat on top. Cover and continue cooking for 30 minutes or until meat and vegetables are done. During last 10 minutes of cooking time, add sauerkraut, caraway seed and pepper. Remove meat and vegetables to hot platter. Serves 6 to 8.

BARLEY SOUP

½ c. medium barley
1 stalk celery, minced
1 medium onion, minced
3 T. butter, melted
1 T. flour
6 c. hot vegetable bouillon
  Salt and pepper to taste
½ c. heavy cream

In a kettle sauté the barley, celery and onion in the melted butter. Stir in flour. Add bouillon. Cover. Simmer 1 hour, or until barley is tender. Season to taste. Just before serving add cream. Do not reheat.

BOILED BEEF

4 lbs. beef chuck	2 carrots
Beef bones	2 stalks celery
Water	1 leek
2 t. salt	2 onions
6 peppercorns	Salt and white
Parsley	pepper to taste

Put beef and bones into a kettle. Add water to cover. Add salt, peppercorns and vegetables. Bring to a boil. Then lower heat and simmer about 3 hours, or until beef is tender. Strain bouillon and season with salt and white pepper to taste. Slice beef and serve with horseradish. Serves 8 to 10.

5

CHOCOLATE TORTE
(SACHERTORTE)

    5 ozs. sweet chocolate, broken in
       small chunks
  ¾ c. butter or margarine
    6 egg yolks, beaten
    6 egg whites
    1 c. powdered sugar
1¼ c. sifted cake flour
  ⅓ c. apricot jam

Melt chocolate in top of a double boiler. Add butter, stirring until melted. Add egg yolks, beating constantly. Add sugar and beat until well mixed. Cool. Beat egg whites until stiff. Fold in chocolate mixture and flour alternately. Pour into a greased 8-inch square pan lined with greased waxed paper. Bake in a preheated 325° oven for 30 minutes or until a toothpick inserted in center comes out clean. Remove from pan. Cool. Melt jam in hot water. Spread on top of cake. Let stand 20 minutes.

FROSTING

    3 ozs. unsweetened chocolate
  ¾ c. powdered sugar
    2 T. hot water
    1 egg
    1 egg yolk
    5 T. butter or margarine

Melt chocolate over hot water. Remove from heat, add sugar and water and beat until well blended. Using a wire whisk, beat mixture into egg. Add egg yolk and beat. Add butter, a tablespoon at a time, beating constantly. Spread on top of the cake. Cool and serve.

VIENNA CHEESECAKE

3 8-oz. pkgs. cream cheese, softened
1 c. plus 2 T. sugar
4 eggs
1 T. vanilla
¼ t. salt
1 c. crushed zwieback crumbs
¼ c. melted butter

Mix softened cream cheese with 1 cup sugar until smooth. Add eggs one at a time while stirring. Add vanilla and salt. Mix crumbs, 2 tablespoons sugar and butter. Pat in bottom of a 9-inch springform pan. Pour in filling. Bake in a 350° oven for 20 minutes. Cool. Spread with pineapple topping. Chill. Remove outer ring and serve.

PINEAPPLE TOPPING

1 9-oz. can crushed pineapple
½ c. sugar
½ c. pineapple juice
3 T. cornstarch
1 egg, beaten
1 T. butter

Combine crushed pineapple, sugar, pineapple juice and cornstarch. Cook over moderate heat, stirring until thick. Add egg and butter. Cook, stirring, a few more minutes. Cool.

Edith Pikelny

JAM POCKETS

1 8-oz. pkg. cream cheese
¼ t. salt
3 T. sugar
1 c. margarine, softened to room
    temperature
2 c. sifted flour
  Apricot jam

Combine first 4 ingredients. Cream until well blended. Work in flour. Chill several hours or overnight. Divide into thirds. Roll out one at a time on a well-floured board to about ⅛-inch thick. Cut into 3-inch squares. Place ½ teaspoon apricot jam in center of each square. Fold so corners overlap in center to enclose jam. Bake on a greased cookie sheet in a 350° oven for about 16 to 18 minutes or until golden brown.

Marcella Borkowski

RASPBERRY TARTLETS

1 c. butter
1 c. powdered sugar
1 egg
1½ t. almond extract
1 t. vanilla
2½ c. sifted all-purpose flour
1 t. salt
  Powdered sugar
  Raspberry jam

Cream butter, gradually add sugar. Beat in egg and extracts. Blend in flour and salt. Chill. Roll dough ⅛-inch thick on a lightly floured surface. Cut with a 1¾-inch round cookie cutter. Cut small hole in center of half of the cookies. Place on lightly greased cookie sheets. Bake in 375° oven about 8 minutes. Cool. Dip cookies with hole in powdered sugar. Spread bottom of whole cookies with a thin layer of raspberry jam. Cover with the sugar-coated cookies, pressing the two together to make a sandwich. Makes about 6½ dozen.

Mary Dixon

CHOCOLATE DROP COOKIES

2 c. sifted flour
1 t. baking powder
¾ c. butter
1 c. powdered sugar
1 egg, well beaten
2 ozs. unsweetened chocolate, melted
1 t. vanilla extract
3 T. cream

Preheat oven to 350°. Mix and sift first 2 ingredients. Cream butter, adding sugar gradually. Beat until fluffy. Add egg, chocolate and vanilla. Mix well. Add dry ingredients alternately with cream to butter mixture. Mix just enough after each addition to combine ingredients. Shape dough into small balls using 2 teaspoons of dough for each ball. Bake on ungreased cookie sheet about 10 minutes. Cool. Frost with the following frosting. Makes about 4½ dozen.

VANILLA FROSTING

2 t. butter, melted
2 t. vanilla
3 T. cream
1½ c. powdered sugar

Combine all ingredients and beat until smooth.

CANADA

BEEF STEW AND DUMPLINGS

2 lbs. beef, cubed	1 c. cubed turnips
2 T. butter	2 small onions, cubed
3 c. boiling water	1 qt. cubed potatoes
1 T. flour	
2 T. cold water	2 t. salt
2 c. cubed carrots	¼ t. pepper

Brown meat in the butter in a large saucepan. Add boiling water. Cover. Simmer about 1¼ hours. Mix flour and water into a paste and add to above mixture. Add carrots, turnips, onions, potatoes and seasonings. Cook 20 minutes. Make the following dumpling recipe. Drop dumplings by spoonsful on stew and cook, covered, about 15 more minutes.

DUMPLINGS

2 c. sifted flour	2 T. butter
4 t. baking powder	1 c. milk
½ t. salt	

Mix and sift first 3 ingredients. Cut in butter into particles about the size of a pea. Add milk. Stir until thick.

Mrs. Ralph W. Cutler

ESCALLOPED OYSTERS

1 pt. oysters
4 T. oyster liquid
2 T. milk or cream
½ c. stale bread crumbs
1 c. cracker crumbs
½ c. melted butter
Salt and pepper to taste

Mix bread and cracker crumbs and stir in butter. Put a thin layer in bottom of a buttered shallow baking dish. Cover with oysters and sprinkle with salt and pepper. Add half of the oyster liquid and half of the milk. Repeat layer. Add remaining oyster liquid and milk. Cover top with remaining crumbs. Bake 30 minutes in a 400° to 450° oven.

Never have more than 2 layers of oysters. If 3 layers are used the middle layer will be underdone and soggy.

Mrs. Alfred C. Ruwe

CREAM OF POTATO SOUP

3 c. diced raw potatoes
½ c. chopped celery
½ c. chopped onion
3 c. water
2 c. scalded milk
2 chicken bouillon cubes
3 T. butter
1 c. sour cream
1 T. flour
Dash of nutmeg (optional)
Salt and pepper to taste
Parsley (optional)

Cook potatoes, celery and onion in the 3 cups of water in a covered pan until tender. Do not drain. Press through a sieve. Add milk, bouillon and butter.

Mix sour cream with flour until smooth. Add to soup. Cook, stirring constantly, until thickened and bouillon cubes are dissolved. Season with salt, pepper and nutmeg. Garnish with parsley if desired.

FRENCH MEAT PIE (TOURTIÈRE)

1½ lbs. pork, ground	½ t. pepper
½ lb. ground beef	1 t. cloves
2 medium onions, minced	1¼ t. cinnamon
	¾ c. water
1 T. salt	

Combine ingredients and brown in a large skillet. Do not overcook. Drain fat. Make upper and lower piecrust for 2 pies. Fill with meat filling. Bake at 400° for 10 minutes, then turn heat down to 350° and bake 40 minutes longer. Serves 4.

This meat pie may be frozen and reheated in the oven before serving.

Mrs. Howard R. Storer

Canada is a country bounded by three oceans and blessed with beautiful lakes and rivers and wide-ranging mountains. Seafood is a favorite in many areas, with English and French foods popular throughout the country.

ANADAMA BREAD

½ c. cornmeal
3 T. shortening
¼ c. molasses
2 t. salt
¾ c. boiling water
1 pkg. active dry yeast (or 1 cake
   compressed)
¼ c. warm water
1 egg, beaten
3 c. sifted all-purpose flour

Combine cornmeal, shortening, molasses, salt and boiling water in a large bowl. Let stand until lukewarm. Sprinkle yeast over warm water to dissolve, then stir yeast, egg and half of the flour into cornmeal mixture. Beat vigorously. Stir in remaining flour and mix thoroughly until dough forms a soft ball. Use your hands if it is easier. Transfer to a greased loaf pan, cover with a cloth. Set in a warm place until dough reaches line above the pan. Sprinkle top with a little cornmeal and salt. Bake at 350° for 50 to 55 minutes. Cool before slicing.

Virginia Kraegenbrink

FRESH APPLE BREAD

2 c. sifted flour
½ t. baking soda
1 t. baking powder
½ t. salt
⅓ c. shortening
1 c. sugar
1 egg
⅓ c. orange juice
¾ c. raisins
¼ c. chopped nuts
1 c. finely chopped apples
1 T. grated orange rind

Sift together flour, soda, baking powder, salt. Cream shortening, sugar and egg. Beat thoroughly. Add dry ingredients alternately with orange juice. Add raisins, nuts, apples, orange rind. Pour into a 9 x 5-inch loaf pan. Bake at 350° for 45 minutes.

Mrs. Herbert Carlson

SAUSAGE CAKE

3 c. brown sugar, firmly packed
1 lb. unseasoned pork sausage
2 eggs, beaten
3¼ c. flour, sifted
¼ t. salt
2 t. baking soda
3 t. baking powder
2 t. cinnamon
1 t. nutmeg
1 c. strong coffee
2 t. vanilla
1 c. raisins
½ c. nuts

Mix sugar with sausage. Add eggs. Mix and sift dry ingredients together. Add to sausage mixture alternately with coffee. Add vanilla and beat well. Add nuts and raisins. Pour in well-greased tube cake pan. Place in cool oven set at 350°. Bake 1½ hours.

DANDELION WINE

1 gal. dandelion blossoms
1 handful dandelion roots, washed
   and scraped
5 lemons, sliced
3 lbs. granulated sugar

Cover dandelion blossoms and roots with boiling water, let stand 24 hours. Strain. If there is not 1 gallon of liquid after straining, add water to make one gallon. Add lemons and sugar. Bring to boiling point, cover, and let stand 14 days. Then strain and bottle. Will keep as long as desired.

Emma Dredla

GREEN TOMATO MINCEMEAT

6 c. chopped tart apples	1 T. cinnamon
6 c. green tomatoes	1 t. powdered cloves
4 c. brown sugar	¾ t. allspice
1⅓ c. vinegar	¾ t. mace
3 c. raisins	¾ t. black pepper
	2 t. salt

Place all ingredients in a large pan and mix. Simmer for 3 hours. Add ¾ cup butter and mix. Pour into scalded pint jars. Seal. Yield: 6 pints.

Ina McCarthy

NEWFOUNDLAND FRUITCAKE

1 lb. margarine	1 lb. dates
½ c. brown sugar	1 c. cherries
1 t. baking soda	1 c. chopped nuts
2½ c. flour	1 t. allspice
3 eggs	1 t. mace
2 t. vanilla	1 t. nutmeg
2 t. maple extract	¼ t. ginger
2 t. almond extract	1 t. cinnamon
½ c. warm water	1 t. cloves
¼ lb. mixed fruit peel	1 c. strawberry jam (optional)
1 lb. raisins	½ c. rum (optional)
1 lb. currants	

Cream butter and sugar. Add eggs and cream well. Add flavoring. Sift flour and spices together. Sprinkle 1 cup flour over fruit and coat well. Add fruit to butter mixture. Add remainder of flour. Add soda which has been dissolved in warm water. If desired, add 1 cup strawberry jam and ½ cup rum. Bake at 375° for 3½ hours.

Mrs. Albert Drodge

CANADA

MOLASSES COOKIES

1 c. bacon fat	2 t. baking soda
1 c. sugar	5½ c. flour
1 c. molasses	2 t. ginger
1 c. hot water	2 t. cinnamon

Cream bacon fat and sugar. Add molasses and hot water in which dissolved baking soda has been added. Sift flour with ginger and cinnamon. Add to molasses mixture. Mix well. Let stand while greasing cookie sheets. (This allows flour to swell, since hot water takes the place of eggs.) Bake at 350° for 12 to 15 minutes. When cool, store in airtight container, putting waxed paper between layers. Yield: 5 dozen cookies.

Gladys Hilpertshauser

MAPLE SYRUP CAKE

½ c. sugar	2¼ c. flour
⅓ c. shortening	3 t. baking powder
¾ c. maple syrup	3 egg whites, beaten
½ c. milk	
Salt to taste	

Cream the sugar and shortening together. Add the syrup and stir well. Add the milk and flour alternately. Fold in the egg whites. Bake in an oblong pan at 350° for 45 to 60 minutes. Remove cake from oven, cool and place on an inverted cake pan. Cover with a favorite frosting.

✓ ORANGE RAISIN CAKE

1 orange	2 c. flour
½ c. sour milk	1½ t. baking powder
1 c. raisins	
½ c. butter	½ t. baking soda
1 c. sugar	½ t. salt
2 eggs	

Add juice of orange to the sour milk. Put skin of orange through a chopper with the raisins. Set aside 2 tablespoons fruit and peel for frosting. Cream the butter, adding sugar gradually. Add the eggs and beat well. Sift together the flour, baking powder, soda and salt and add alternately with the milk and orange juice. Fold in the raisin and orange mixture. Turn into a 9 x 9-inch greased pan and bake 1 hour in a 350° oven. Frost with a butter icing to which the leftover fruit and peel mixture has been added.

Margaret Gardner

✓ AMBROSIA PIE

1 c. crushed cornflakes
4 T. melted butter
1 can sweetened condensed milk
1 14-oz. can fruit cocktail, drained
⅓ c. lemon juice

Mix cornflakes and butter together. Put in bottom and sides of pie plate. Save 2 tablespoons of the mixture for the top.

Mix together remaining ingredients. Pour over crumbs. Put whipped topping or whipped cream over fruit. Sprinkle with remaining crumbs. Chill 8 hours.

Darlene Bartsch

OAT CAKES

3 c. rolled oats	½ t. salt
3 c. flour	2 c. shortening
1 c. sugar	½ c. cold water

Combine the rolled oats, flour, sugar and salt in a large bowl. Cut in the shortening or work it in with your hands until the dough is manageable. Moisten with cold water. Roll, not too thin, using rolled oats on the board to prevent the dough from sticking. Cut into desired shapes, or use a knife and cut into diamonds or squares. Bake in a 350° oven for 15 minutes. Yield: 6 to 7 dozen cakes.

Margaret Gardner

CHINA

SWEET AND SOUR PORK

1½ lbs. lean pork
2 T. fat
¼ c. water
¾ c. green pepper, cut in strips
¼ c. onion, sliced
2½ c. pineapple chunks, drained
¼ c. brown sugar
2 T. cornstarch
½ t. salt
⅓ c. vinegar
1 T. soy sauce
½ c. slivered almonds (optional)
1 c. pineapple juice
   Cooked rice

Cut pork into strips 2 inches long and ½-inch wide. Brown in hot fat. Add water, cover and cook in an electric skillet for 1 hour. Add pepper strips, onion slices and pineapple and sauté. Combine brown sugar, cornstarch, salt, vinegar, pineapple juice and soy sauce. Mix and cook until slightly thickened, stirring constantly. Pour over hot cooked pork, cover and simmer 10 minutes. Serve over cooked rice. Garnish with almonds.

Mrs. Herman Matzick

CANTONESE SHRIMP

3 c. hot cooked rice
12 ozs. peeled, deveined raw shrimp, halved lengthwise
2 T. butter or margarine
2 c. diagonally sliced celery
2 c. sliced onions
½ lb. fresh spinach
1 16-oz. can Chinese vegetables, drained
¼ t. pepper
¼ c. soy sauce
1¼ c. chicken broth
2 T. cornstarch

In a large skillet, sauté shrimp in the butter for 1 minute or until shrimp turn pink. Add celery and onions. Cook 2 minutes, stirring constantly. Add spinach and Chinese vegetables. Cover and cook 1 minute. Blend pepper, soy sauce, chicken broth and cornstarch. Stir into above mixture. Cook until sauce is clear and thick, about 2 minutes. Stir while cooking. Serve over rice. Yield: 6 servings.

ALMOND CHICKEN

¾ t. salt
½ t. Accent
2 T. cornstarch
3 T. soy sauce
1 t. sugar
3 T. peanut oil or salad oil
¼ c. chicken broth
1 c. celery, diced
1 c. onion, diced
1 c. canned bamboo shoots
8 water chestnuts, sliced (optional)
1 lb. uncooked chicken, diced
2 T. sherry
½ lb. almonds, walnuts or cashews

Dredge chicken in the mixture of salt, Accent, cornstarch, soy sauce and sugar. Marinate ½ hour. Heat a skillet. Add oil and sauté chicken until tender. Add chicken broth and heat thoroughly. Sauté all vegetables slightly and add to the chicken mixture with the sherry and nuts. Serve hot. Serves 4 to 6.

Fran Wong Berry

BEEF AND SNOW PEAS

3 T. peanut oil or salad oil
1 clove garlic
1 lb. flank or sirloin steak, sliced thin
1 large onion, sliced
1 lb. fresh snow peas (or two 6-oz. frozen cartons, thawed)
1 T. cornstarch
2 T. soy sauce
1 cube beef bouillon (dissolved in ½ c. water)
1 t. salt
½ c. water
1 t. sugar (optional)
½ t. Accent

Pour oil in a skillet. Bring to a boil. Add garlic and fry. Remove from skillet. Add beef. Sauté until meat is brown, then remove. Fry onion. Add pea pods. Cook about 5 minutes. Add mixture of cornstarch, soy sauce and remaining ingredients to vegetables and meat. Cook until gravy thickens, stirring slowly. Serves 6 to 8.

Wyla Wong

SHANGHAI CASSEROLE

1 lb. lean ground beef
1 t. each onion and garlic powders
1 c. sliced celery
1 c. cooked mixed vegetables
1 10¾-oz. can condensed cream of
  mushroom soup, undiluted
3 c. cooked rice
2 T. soy sauce
¼ t. pepper
1 c. Chinese noodles

Brown meat with onion and garlic powders in a lightly greased skillet. Add celery, mixed vegetables, soup. Stir in rice and seasonings. Turn into a greased 2-quart casserole. Cover and bake at 350° for 25 minutes. Uncover. Top with noodles. Bake uncovered 5 more minutes. Serves 6.

EGG ROLLS

¾ c. sifted flour   2 eggs, beaten
1 T. cornstarch   1½ c. water
½ t. salt   ¼ c. melted butter
¼ t. sugar

Preheat a 6-inch skillet. Combine above ingredients and blend thoroughly. Pour ¼ cup batter for each pancake into hot skillet. Cover entire bottom of skillet with the batter. Brown on each side. Fill each pancake with ¼ cup of the following hot filling. Roll as for a jelly roll. Seal edge with a paste made with 1 tablespoon flour and 2 tablespoons water. Melt ¼ cup butter in a skillet. Cook egg rolls on both sides until brown. Serve hot.

FILLING

½ c. chopped celery
¾ c. chopped cabbage
¼ c. water
1 4½-oz. can shrimp, drained
½ c. cooked, diced chicken or pork
½ c. minced green onion tops
1 5-oz. can water chestnuts,
  drained and chopped
1 clove garlic
3 T. butter, melted
¼ c. soy sauce

Cook celery and cabbage in water until tender. Drain. Add shrimp, chicken or pork, onion, chestnuts and garlic to the butter. Brown slightly. Add soy sauce and cook 5 more minutes. Add celery and cabbage. Mix.

HONG KONG CASSEROLE

1 can cream of mushroom soup
½ c. evaporated milk
1 12-oz. can shrimp
1 large can button mushrooms
1 small pkg. frozen peas
1 c. diced celery
1 large can chow mein noodles
1 t. instant onion
¼ c. blanched almonds (or cashews)
  Dash of bitters

Mix all ingredients together lightly, reserving enough chow mein noodles for topping. Pour into greased casserole. Top with reserved noodles. Bake at 350° for 45 minutes. Serves 6.

Margaret Gardner

Just as America has its own regional ways of preparing food, so Chinese cooking is divided into local regions, the most widely recognized being Canton or Peking. Vegetables are rarely served separately but are included in the main dish.

ALMOND COOKIES

2½ c. sifted all-purpose flour
¾ c. sugar
¼ t. salt
1 t. double-acting baking powder
¾ c. soft shortening or lard
1 egg
2 T. water
1 t. almond extract

Mix shortening with egg until creamy. Add water and almond extract. Mix well. Gradually add sifted dry ingredients, stirring with fork until mixture draws away from sides of bowl. Blend with hands. Refrigerate 1 hour. Shape into 1-inch balls and place on a greased cookie sheet. Flatten with palm of hand to ¼-inch thickness. Press half an almond in each if desired. Bake in a preheated 350° oven 25 minutes or until golden. Makes 3 dozen cookies.

CZECHOSLOVAKIA

PECAN BUTTER CRESCENTS

1 c. butter or margarine
2 c. flour
1 egg yolk, slightly beaten
½ pt. sour cream
1 12-oz. can fruit filling
Powdered sugar

Cut butter into flour as for pie dough. Combine egg yolk with sour cream and add to flour mixture. Form into a ball and wrap in waxed paper. Chill overnight. Divide into four portions. Roll each into a 12-inch circle. Spread fruit filling evenly over entire circle. Cut into 16 wedges. Roll from wide end to form crescents. Bake on ungreased cookie sheet at 375° for 20 minutes, or until delicately browned. Dust with powdered sugar when cool.

Mildred Tesinsky

POPPY SEED CAKE

6 eggs, separated	½ t. cream of tartar
1½ c. sugar	½ c. cold water
1½ c. flour	1 t. vanilla
¼ t. salt	¾ c. poppy seed

Add salt to egg whites and beat until foamy, then add the cream of tartar and beat until stiff. Add ½ cup of the sugar. Beat well and set aside. Then beat the egg yolks, add 1 cup of sugar and beat well. Add cold water to this mixture and beat until lemon colored. Add flour, beat well. Fold into the egg whites. Fold in poppy seed carefully. Pour into an ungreased angel food pan and bake at 325° 1 hour. Invert, until cool. When cool, cut into two layers. Put a butter cream frosting between layers.

KOLACHES

- 6 T. lukewarm milk
- 2 pkgs. active dry yeast (or 2 cakes compressed yeast)
- 1 t. salt
- 2 T. sugar
- ½ c. soft butter
- 4 eggs
- 4 egg yolks
- 4 c. all-purpose flour

Add yeast to milk and let stand several minutes to dissolve. Stir in salt and sugar. Put butter in a large bowl, adding 1 whole egg and 1 egg yolk, and beating very hard. Continue adding 1 whole egg and additional yolk, followed each time by hard beating. When all the eggs have been used, mix in yeast and then flour, beating hard. Cover with a towel and place in a warm place until double in size. Pinch off pieces of dough the size of a large walnut. Place 2 inches apart on a greased baking sheet, cover, and let rise in a warm place for 30 minutes. Press a hollow in the center of each piece with your fingers and fill the cavity with prune filling, jam or marmalade.

Bake in a preheated 350° oven 20 to 25 minutes. Remove from oven. When cool sprinkle top generously with sugar.

FILLING

- 1 lb. prunes, cooked
- 1 T. sugar
- 1 T. butter, softened
- ½ t. cinnamon
- ½ t. vanilla

When prunes are tender drain, discarding pits and chopping coarsely. Stir in sugar, butter, cinnamon and vanilla. Add more sugar if desired.

Virginia Kraegenbrink

SAUTÉED MUSHROOMS

- 6 T. butter, melted
- ½ c. finely chopped onions
- 1 lb. fresh mushrooms, thinly sliced
- ½ t. caraway seed
- Salt to taste

Fry onions in the melted butter. Cook 4 to 6 minutes, or until translucent, then add mushrooms, caraway seed and salt. Sauté 10 to 15 minutes. Serves 4.

SOUR BEEF AND POTATO DUMPLINGS

- 4 lbs. beef
- 2 c. white vinegar
- 4 c. water
- 1 medium onion, cut up
- 1 T. salt
- ½ c. raisins
- 1 heaping t. pickling spice (in cloth bag)
- ½ c. white sugar
- ¼ c. brown sugar
- 14 gingersnaps

Cut beef in serving pieces and combine with vinegar, water, onion, salt, raisins and spices in a large pot. Simmer about 1 hour. Add sugars and 8 to 10 gingersnaps, broken up. Simmer another ¾ hour, stirring occasionally. Add remaining gingersnaps and stir until dissolved. When meat is done, prepare dumplings.

DUMPLINGS

6 baking potatoes	2 eggs,
1 t. salt	well beaten
½ c. bread crumbs	1 c. flour

Rice potatoes. Add salt, bread crumbs and beaten eggs; then add flour. Place buttered brown bread cubes in center of each dumpling. Drop in boiling salted water. Boil until they rise to top.

Eleanor Brandt

CZECHOSLOVAKIA

The one feature of Czechoslovakian food is the dumpling, served with meat as a main course or a fruit filling for dessert. Of all vegetables, mushrooms are the most popular.

DENMARK

DANISH SANDWICHES

FAIRYLAND FANTASY

Arrange 3 or 4 slices "boiled" ham on lettuce, folding and overlapping slices. Top with 2 cooked prunes stuffed with cream cheese and separated with thin, twisted orange slice.

JUTLAND JUBILEE

Blend 1 tablespoon horse-radish with 3 tablespoons cream cheese and spread on 3 slices chopped ham, lunch-eon meat or honeyloaf. Form slices in rolls and place on lettuce, separating rolls with 3 thin apple wedges dipped in lemon juice. Garnish with mayonnaise and chopped nuts.

COPENHAGEN CLOVERLEAF

Place 2 to 4 slices salami flat on lettuce, then 3 slices folded and arranged in cloverleaf pattern. Top each with slice of cucumber and hard-cooked egg. Garnish with pimiento and parsley.

Located on the northern tip of Europe, Denmark is famed for its open-face sandwiches of hundreds of varieties, each sandwich heaped with delectable foods in interesting combinations.

LEMON BREAD

1 c. sugar	1 t. baking
6 T. butter	powder
2 eggs	Rind of 1 lemon
½ c. milk	Pinch of salt
1½ c. flour	

Mix all ingredients together. Put in loaf pan. Bake at 375° for 1 hour, until done. Drizzle the following glaze over the hot bread: Mix juice of 1 lemon and ⅓ cup sugar. Stir occasionally while bread is baking.

Marcia Madsen Hays

DANISH SANDWICHES

ROYAL ROAST BEEF

Place 3 to 5 slices rare or medium roast beef on lettuce bed. Arrange 3 bacon curls in diagonal row across top. Put 1 tablespoon egg salad in each space between curls. Garnish with thin wedges of tomato and green pepper.

TIVOLI TEMPTER

Spread bread with thick layer of liver sausage and garnish edge with chopped parsley. Arrange diagonally across top 3 onion rings and 3 slices mushrooms. Garnish with bacon curl and cherry tomato stuffed with cream cheese.

DANISH LUNCH

Top lettuce with 2 slices cooked pork. Top with 2 diagonally folded slices, pointing in opposite directions. Put 2 tablespoons potato salad in center and slip 2 green pepper rings under folds of top slices of pork. Garnish.

PORK TENDERLOIN

1 pork tenderloin
5 T. butter
3 medium onions, sliced thin

Cut tenderloin in four serving pieces and pound flat. Sauté in 2 of the tablespoons of butter until lightly brown. Add some water and cook until well done, about 20 to 25 minutes. Sauté the onions in remaining butter until dark brown. Drain. Serve over tenderloin slices. Serves 4.

DATE NUT BREAD

1 c. chopped dates	4 c. flour
2 t. baking soda	2 t. baking powder
2 c. boiling water	1 t. salt
2 or more T. butter	2 t. vanilla
1½ c. sugar	1 c. ground nuts
2 eggs	2 large ripe bananas

Mix above ingredients in a large bowl. Bake in 2 single loaf pans at 350° for 1 hour.

Golda C. Neighbours

ENGLAND

ENGLISH MINCEMEAT

Make this mincemeat in October and put in a stone crock in a cold cellar. Stir once a week until Thanksgiving.

- 2 lbs. seedless black raisins, chopped
- 2 lbs. currants, chopped
- 4 qts. apples, peeled and chopped
- 2 lbs. kidney suet, chopped
- ½ lb. lemon peel, chopped
- ¼ lb. citron, chopped
- 2 lbs. dark brown sugar
- 3 t. each: cinnamon, allspice, nutmeg
- 1 pt. apple cider

Mix all ingredients in an enameled kettle or bowl and transfer to a stone crock. Cover and let stand to age in a cold cellar. Stir once a week until Thanksgiving so ingredients are well blended. It will keep indefinitely if kept very cold.

Mrs. J. D. O'Neill

HOT SPICED TEA

- 1 c. sugar
- 1 c. water
- 12 whole cloves
- 2 1-inch sticks cinnamon

Put above ingredients in a saucepan and bring to a boil. Remove from heat, cover and let stand 20 or 30 minutes. Reheat and boil again. Add 3 teaspoons tea and steep for 5 minutes. Strain into the following mixture:

2 qts. water	½ c. lemon juice
¾ c. orange juice	1 c. pineapple juice

Heat and serve. Yield: 20 cups.

Lucille Pearce

ENGLISH PLUM BREAD

- 2 c. milk
- 1 c. water
- 2 yeast cakes (dissolved in a little water)
- 8 c. flour
- 1 lb. raisins, halved
- 4 ozs. citron, sliced very thin
- ½ c. sugar

Scald milk and water and cool until warm. Add yeast. Add flour to make dough stiff enough to knead. Cover. Let rise until it reaches top of bowl. Cut raisins and citron into dough with sugar. Let rise again. Mold into mounds and put in bread pans. Let rise again. Bake in a 350° oven until brown, then reduce heat and bake for about 1 hour. Makes 2 large loaves.

Mrs. Kermit Stevens

FINNAN HADDIE WITH RICE (KEDGEREE)

- 6 T. butter or margarine
- 1½ c. cooked rice
- 1½ c. cooked flaked smoked haddock
- 3 hard-cooked eggs, chopped
  Salt and pepper to taste
- 2 T. chopped parsley

Heat butter until golden. Add all ingredients except parsley. Cook over low heat until heated through, stirring occasionally. Garnish with parsley.

CHEF SALAD

- ¼ c. vinegar
- 2 T. dry vermouth
- 1 envelope old-fashioned French salad dressing mix
- ⅔ c. salad oil
- 2 T. chopped parsley
- 8 c. bite-size pieces salad greens
- 1 c. boiled ham strips
- 1 c. cheddar cheese strips

Combine vinegar and vermouth in a jar with a tight-fitting lid. Add salad dressing mix. Cover and shake well. Add salad oil and parsley. Cover and shake again. Place salad greens, ham and cheese in a large bowl. Add prepared salad dressing and toss lightly. Makes 10 to 12 servings.

BEEF RIB ROAST

2- to 4-rib beef rib roast
Salt and pepper to taste

Have the butcher remove the backbone (for easier carving) and tie roast. Season meat with salt and pepper. Place roast, fat side up, on a rack in an open roasting pan. Insert roast meat thermometer so bulb is centered in the thickest part, making sure bulb does not rest in fat or on bone. Do not add water. Do not cover. Roast at 325° to desired degree of doneness. (The meat thermometer will register 140° for rare; 160° for medium; 170° for well done. Allow 23 to 25 minutes per pound for rare; 27 to 30 minutes for medium; 32 to 35 for well done.) Roasts are more easily carved if they "stand" 15 to 20 minutes after removing from oven. Because roasts continue to cook after removal from oven (unless they are carved and served immediately), remove roast when thermometer registers about 5 degrees below temperature indication desired. Serve with Individual Yorkshire Puddings.

INDIVIDUAL YORKSHIRE PUDDINGS

1 c. sifted flour	1 c. milk
¾ t. salt	2 T. drippings
2 eggs	

About 15 minutes before roast is done, increase oven temperature to 400°. Sift together flour and salt. Beat eggs and combine with milk. Slowly add dry ingredients, beating constantly. Remove roast from oven and spoon off about ¼ cup clear hot beef drippings. Place ½ teaspoon beef drippings in each of 12 preheated large muffin pans. Pour about 2 tablespoons pudding batter into each. Bake for 30 minutes or until golden brown. Serve with roast. Heat remaining juices in roasting pan and serve over puddings if desired.

General Foods

CODFISH BALLS

6 medium potatoes
2 c. codfish, shredded
2 eggs
½ c. milk
  Salt and pepper to taste

Boil potatoes, then pare and mash. Add fish and eggs. Blend. Add milk and seasonings. Beat until fluffy. Drop from a spoon into deep hot fat and fry 10 minutes. Drain on absorbent paper. Yield: 6 servings.

BAKED FISH AND CHIPS

1 lb. fish fillets
1 envelope seasoned coating mix for fish
1 16-oz. pkg. frozen French fried potatoes
  Salt to taste

Coat fish with seasoned coating mix as directed on package. Arrange in a single layer on a greased baking sheet. Spread potatoes in a single layer on separate baking sheet or shallow pan. Bake potatoes on top of oven rack at 450° for 5 minutes. Then place fish on lower oven rack and bake with potatoes until both are golden brown, about 15 minutes. Season potatoes with salt. Serve fish and potatoes immediately. Makes 4 servings.

VEAL PIE

1 c. onions, finely chopped
1 T. shortening
1 lb. ground veal
1 T. flour
1 c. milk
1 t. salt
¼ t. black pepper
¼ c. chopped parsley
3 egg yolks
1 c. sour cream
⅔ c. flour
½ t. salt
3 egg whites
1½ c. shredded cheddar cheese

Fry the onions gently in the shortening until clear but not brown. Add the veal and the 1 tablespoon flour and fry until lightly brown, stirring gently. Stir in the milk, salt and pepper and simmer until thick. Stir in parsley and remove from heat.

Blend together in a mixing bowl the egg yolks and sour cream. Then beat well. Stir in the ⅔ cup flour and the ½ teaspoon salt. Beat the egg whites until stiff and fold gently into the egg yolk mixture.

Pour half of the egg mixture into a well-greased 9-inch pie pan or a shallow casserole. Top with half of the cheese. Bake in a 400° oven 10 minutes. Remove from the oven and gently place the veal mixture on top. Spread carefully. Pour the remaining egg mixture over the veal and bake 10 or 15 minutes longer until golden brown. Top with the remaining cheese and place in oven for a few minutes to melt. Serve hot with sour cream if desired. Serves 4 to 6.

Mrs. J. Davidson

YORKSHIRE HOT POT

4 shoulder lamb chops
1 garlic clove, minced
4 small whole onions
4 medium potatoes, halved and pared
1 pkg. frozen cut beans
¼ to ½ t. ground cloves
2 t. salt
  Pepper to taste
1 can cream of mushroom soup
½ can water
  Paprika

Brown chops in a heavy skillet with garlic. Tuck onions and potatoes around and under chops. Add beans, cloves, salt, pepper, soup and water. Cover. Cook slowly 1 hour. Thicken and sprinkle with paprika.

Mrs. H. Kunnemann

CHOCOLATE BISCUIT CAKE

1 lb. biscuits (cookies)
¾ c. margarine
4 ozs. block chocolate
2 T. sugar
2 T. golden syrup
2 T. cocoa powder

Crumble biscuits (cookies) and roll out finely. Mix together well the sugar, margarine and syrup until mixture is creamy. Work in cocoa and then stir in biscuit crumbs.

Spread mixture into a flat tin and cover with Chocolate Cream. Sprinkle with grated chocolate. Place in refrigerator or a cold place for 2 hours. Cut and serve.

CHOCOLATE CREAM

¼ lb. butter or margarine
3 ozs. finely granulated sugar
2 ozs. chocolate or cocoa
3 T. milk

Cream butter well and add remaining ingredients, then beat thoroughly until creamy.

Mrs. P. Monaghan

Proud of its rivers, lakes and coastal waters, England's most popular dishes are made with sole, mackerel and cod. Today fish and chips compete with the traditional roast beef as the national dish.

CRUMPETS

2 pkgs. active dry yeast
1 t. sugar
½ c. lukewarm water
2 eggs, beaten
1½ c. lukewarm milk
2 T. melted butter or margarine
½ t. salt
3 c. sifted flour

Preheat oven to 400°. In a small shallow bowl sprinkle yeast and sugar over the lukewarm water and let stand for 4 or 5 minutes. Then stir together to dissolve the yeast. Add the beaten eggs, milk, butter and salt. Add the yeast and sugar mixture and the flour, beating until smooth. Cover and let rise in a warm place for about 15 minutes. Fill greased muffin pans half full. Bake 10 to 15 minutes or until done. Serve with unsalted butter, syrup, or a favorite jam, jelly or marmalade.

APPLE PIE

8 to 10 baking apples, pared, cored and quartered
4 cloves
¼ lb. sugar
1 T. water
Peel of ½ lemon, grated
Dash of nutmeg

Place apples as close together as possible in a pie dish. Sprinkle with cloves, sugar, lemon peel, a little lemon juice and nutmeg. Add water. Cover. Bake in a 350° oven about 1¼ hours.

Mary Alice Campbell

ROSE HIP PUREE

Pear-shaped cylinders, prickly red,
Festoon the quiescent bushes.
Haunting fragrance accompanies
The harvesting of gaudy bells.

Deblossom, boil and press the fruit.
Boil and press again. Sweeten
With nectar's yield, amber honey
Stored in full combs while roses bloomed.

Spread on hot potato biscuits
Or eat for dessert like a sauce.
Seal some into sterilized jars
For a winter taste of summer.

And when your country roses bloom,
Even though they lack perfume,
You'll anticipate the harvest boon,
Of rose hip puree with tea.

Marylin Barr

ENGLISH TRIFLE

1 packaged jelly roll
1 6-oz. pkg. cherry gelatin
1 1-lb. can fruit cocktail, drained
Whipped cream
Chopped walnuts

Slice the jelly roll in ½-inch to 1-inch slices and cover the bottom of a 9 x 13-inch pan.

Prepare the gelatin according to directions on the package and allow to set slightly. Stir in the fruit cocktail and pour over the jelly roll.

Top with whipped cream and sprinkle with chopped walnuts in amounts desired.

Chill until gelatin is firm. Cut in squares and serve.

Mrs. George W. Banning

FRANCE

CHICKEN MARENGO

½ t. salt
1 t. paprika
¼ t. pepper
1 3-lb. frying chicken, quartered
3 T. butter
¼ c. chopped onion
½ c. dry white wine
1 c. sliced, fresh mushrooms
1 10½-oz. can condensed cream of
   chicken soup
⅛ t. tabasco
¼ c. currant jelly

Sprinkle chicken with seasonings. Then brown in 2 tablespoons butter in a skillet. Add onion and ¼ cup wine. Cook, covered, until tender, about 30 minutes. Cook mushrooms in remaining butter, then add with remaining ingredients to chicken. Mix well and heat thoroughly. Makes 4 servings.

France . . . possessing three coastlines and a mountainous southeast, is a country where cooking is treated as a fine art. Notable French cuisine includes the rémoulade, omelet, soufflé, consommé and crêpe.

FRENCH OMELET

3 eggs
3 T. water
¼ t. salt
⅛ t. pepper
¼ t. basil, thyme, oregano, or parsley
   flakes
1 T. butter or margarine

Mix eggs, water, salt, pepper and desired herb with a fork. Heat butter or margarine in a skillet or 8-inch pan just hot enough to sizzle a drop of water. Pour in egg mixture. It should set at edges at once. Reduce heat slightly but cook eggs quickly. As the mixture at the edges thickens, draw these portions with the fork toward the center so that the uncooked portions flow to the bottom. Tilt skillet, as it is necessary to hasten flow of uncooked eggs. Shake skillet to keep omelet sliding freely. Keep mixture as level as possible. When eggs are set and surface is still moist, increase heat to brown bottom quickly. Roll out or fold on serving plate. Makes 1 or 2 servings.

FRENCH BREAD

1 pkg. dry yeast
1¼ c. lukewarm water
1½ t. salt
1 T. melted butter
1 T. sugar
3¾ c. sifted flour
   Yellow cornmeal
   Sesame seeds

Dissolve yeast in water. Add sugar, salt, butter and 3½ cups flour and beat well. Place ¼ cup flour on a board and knead until smooth and elastic. Place in a greased bowl. Cover. Let rise in a warm place until doubled. Punch down. Let rise again until doubled. Divide dough into 2 parts. Shape each part into a 14-inch loaf, tapered at each end. Place on a baking sheet sprinkled with cornmeal. Let rise, uncovered, until doubled. Brush glaze over loaves. Sprinkle with sesame seeds. Make several diagonal slashes ¼-inch deep across the tops of the loaves. Place a large shallow pan of hot water on lower shelf of oven. Place bread on upper shelf. Bake in a preheated 400° oven about 35 minutes. Remove bread from pans and brush with glaze again.

Glaze

1 t. cornstarch
½ c. plus 1 t. water
¼ t. salt

Combine cornstarch, salt, water. Stir and cook until clear.

FRENCH ONION SOUP
(SOUPE À L'OIGNON)

3 T. butter
2 c. sliced onion
6 beef bouillon cubes
6 c. boiling water
¼ c. grated parmesan cheese

Sauté the onion in the butter until light brown. Dissolve bouillon cubes in the boiling water. Add to cooked onion and simmer about 15 minutes. Serve hot. Sprinkle with parmesan cheese. Serves 8.

FRENCH OVEN BEEF STEW

  2 lbs. beef, cut in 1½-inch cubes
  2 medium onions, cut in eighths
  3 stalks celery, cut in diagonal pieces
  4 medium carrots, cut in half crosswise
     and lengthwise
  1 c. tomato juice
 ⅓ c. quick-cooking tapioca
  1 T. sugar
  1 T. salt
 ¼ t. pepper
 ½ t. basil
  2 medium red potatoes, cut in slices
     ¼-inch thick

Combine beef, onion, celery, carrots, tomato juice, tapioca, sugar, salt, pepper and basil in a 2½-quart casserole. Cover and cook in a 300° oven for 2½ hours. Mix potatoes into stew and cook uncovered 1 hour longer. Stir occasionally. Serves 8.

LOBSTER NEWBURG

3 boiled lobster tails, diced
4 T. butter or margarine
1½ c. sherry wine
1½ c. heavy cream
3 egg yolks
½ t. powdered mustard
½ t. ground basil
Salt and white pepper to taste

Heat lobster in the butter over low heat. Do not brown. Add wine and cook about 5 minutes, until wine is almost absorbed. Add cream and egg yolks, beaten together. Stir constantly until sauce is thickened. Season with salt, pepper, mustard and basil. Serve from a chafing dish on small patty shells or on toast points.

SHRIMP RÉMOULADE

2 lbs. cooked, cleaned large shrimp
2 c. mayonnaise
½ c. brown mustard
¼ c. catsup
4 t. horseradish
2 t. Worcestershire sauce
3 T. lemon juice
1 t. hot pepper sauce
¾ c. chopped parsley
½ c. chopped green onions
1 c. minced celery heart
¼ c. drained capers

Combine all ingredients except shrimp. Blend well. Chill several hours. Serve with hot shrimp.

FRENCH COOKIES

2 c. brown sugar
3 c. flour
1 c. hot water (with 1 t. baking soda)
1 t. cinnamon
1 t. baking powder
2 eggs
1 c. melted shortening
1 c. raisins or nuts

Put all ingredients in a bowl. Do not stir until all ingredients are added. Bake on large greased and floured flat baking sheet in 350° oven for 20 to 25 minutes. Cut in squares when cool land frost.

Mrs. Larry L. Jessen

DESSERT PANCAKES
(CRÊPES SUZETTE)

1 c. sifted flour
2 eggs
1½ c. milk
2 T. melted butter or margarine
Salt to taste
Sugar to taste

Beat flour, eggs and milk until smooth. Add butter, salt, sugar. Let batter stand at least 2 hours. Heat a well-greased 6-inch skillet. Add batter to cover bottom of pan with a thin layer. Brown each side. Grease pan after cooking each pancake. Roll as cooked. Stack pancakes between waxed paper. Makes 2 dozen.

CRÈME BRÛLÉE

1 3¼-oz. pkg. vanilla pudding and pie filling
1½ c. milk
2 pears, peeled and sliced thin
1 10-oz. pkg. frozen raspberries, thawed and drained
2 c. sour cream
½ c. firmly packed light brown sugar

Cook pudding according to directions on package, using 1½ cups milk. Pour into a 1-quart shallow baking dish. Chill until firm. When ready to serve, arrange pears on top of pudding and top with raspberries. Spread sour cream evenly over fruit. Sprinkle with brown sugar. Broil 3 inches from heat for 1 to 2 minutes, or until sugar caramelizes.

CRÈME CHARLOTTE

2 c. boiling milk
5 egg yolks
⅔ c. sugar
1 c. boiling water
1½ envelopes unflavored gelatin
2 c. heavy cream, whipped
½ c. mixed candied fruit
Grand Marnier to taste

On top half of a double boiler, cream egg yolks with sugar until frothy. Slowly pour milk into egg mixture, beating constantly. Place top half of double boiler over bottom pan containing the boiling water. Beat until egg mixture is cooked. Remove from heat and add Grand Marnier. Then add gelatin. Continue beating until cold. Fold in whipped cream. Add candied fruit. Cool in refrigerator.

GERMANY

PORK LOIN ROAST

Place a 4- to 6-pound pork loin roast, fat side up, on a rack in an open roasting pan. Insert roast meat thermometer so the bulb is centered in the thickest part. Make certain bulb does not rest in fat or on bone. Do not add water. Do not cover. Roast in a slow 325° oven until the thermometer registers 170°. Allow 30 to 35 minutes per pound for roasting a center loin; 35 to 40 minutes per pound for a half loin; 40 to 45 minutes per pound for an end roast (total time—2 to 3 hours).

Note: Have the butcher loosen the chine (back) bone by sawing across the rib bones. When roasting is finished, the backbone can be removed easily by running the carving knife along the edge of the roast before the meat is placed on the platter to be carved.

PORK GRAVY

¼ c. pork drippings
3 T. flour
2 c. water
  Salt and pepper to taste

Remove roast from pan and place on carving board. Pour off all but ¼ cup drippings, leaving brown particles in pan. Blend flour and cook, stirring constantly, over low heat until mixture is lightly browned. Remove from heat. Gradually add water, blending well after each addition. Return to heat. Bring to a boil, stirring constantly, and continue cooking until mixture thickens. Cook slowly 3 to 5 minutes, stirring occasionally. Season to taste with salt and pepper.

GERMAN DISH

2 c. sauerkraut
1 16-oz. can applesauce
½ c. dry wine
2 T. brown sugar
1 8-oz. can onions
9 Polish sausages
2 c. drained potatoes, boiled

Combine all ingredients. Simmer 20 minutes.

Loretta Hesterwerth

APPLE-KRAUT HAYSTACKS

4 to 6 slices bacon
4 large tart apples
1 can (1-lb. 11-oz.) sauerkraut, drained
1 t. salt
½ t. caraway seed

Cut apples in half crosswise. Remove core and seeds from center portion. Place halves, cut side down, in a baking pan. Add 2 tablespoons water. Bake at 350° for 20 minutes. Cut bacon in ½-inch pieces. Pan fry until crisp. Drain on absorbent paper. Add bacon drippings, salt and caraway seed to sauerkraut. Remove apples from oven, turn with hollow side up and fill with approximately ½ cup sauerkraut mixture. Return to oven and bake 10 minutes longer or until heated through. Remove from oven and sprinkle top with bacon pieces. Serves 8.

SAUSAGE STUFFING BALLS

1 lb. fresh pork sausage
1 8-oz. pkg. seasoned stuffing mix
¾ c. hot water
½ c. finely chopped onion
½ c. finely chopped celery
1 egg, beaten
½ t. baking powder

Combine stuffing mix with hot water. Break sausage into small pieces and add to moistened stuffing mix. Stir in onion, celery, egg and baking powder until evenly distributed. Shape into balls, using ¼ cup mixture for each ball, and place in baking pan. Cover with foil, securing tightly around pan. Bake in a 325° oven 15 minutes. Remove foil; increase oven temperature to 350° and continue baking 25 minutes or until sausage is done. Makes 18 to 22 balls.

RED CABBAGE WITH APPLE

2 16-oz. jars sweet-sour red cabbage
1 medium tart red apple, cut in thin wedges and halved
1 medium onion, halved and sliced
¼ c. raisins
½ t. caraway seed

Combine cabbage, apple, onion, raisins and caraway seed in a skillet or saucepan. Bring to a boil, cover and reduce heat. Cook slowly for 15 minutes or until apple is tender and raisins are plump. Drain if desired. Makes 6 servings.

VEAL CUTLET WITH SOUR CREAM
(RAHMSCHNITZEL)

1 lb. thinly sliced veal cutlets
1 T. all-purpose flour
¼ t. salt
2 T. butter or margarine
1 10-oz. pkg. frozen Bavarian-style beans and noodles in sauce
1 T. all-purpose flour
½ c. water
1 chicken bouillon cube
½ c. sour cream
½ t. lemon juice (optional)

Pound veal cutlets between sheets of waxed paper until very thin. Sprinkle lightly with 1 tablespoon flour and the salt. Sauté in butter in a large skillet until tender and golden brown on both sides. Place on serving platter. Keep warm. Prepare vegetables as directed on package. Keep warm.

Blend 1 tablespoon flour into drippings in skillet. Add water and bouillon cube. Bring to a boil over medium heat. Blend in sour cream and lemon juice. Simmer until slightly thickened, about 2 to 3 minutes. Strain and pour over veal cutlets. Serve with vegetables. Garnish with chopped parsley and lemon slices or capers if desired. Makes 3 or 4 servings.

CHEDDAR CHEESE SOUP

1½ c. diced potatoes
1 c. chopped onion
1 t. salt
2 beef bouillon cubes
2 c. water
1 c. beer
¼ lb. grated cheddar cheese

Combine first 5 ingredients in a covered pan and simmer until vegetables are tender, about 10 to 15 minutes. Pour into blender and puree. Return to pan and add cheese, stirring over low heat until cheese melts. Gradually whisk in the beer and stir until it is well mixed into the cheese. Serve hot. Yield: 4 to 6 servings.

Charlene Myers

GERMAN PANCAKE

3 eggs   ½ c. milk
½ c. flour   2 T. melted butter
¼ t. salt   Powdered sugar

Combine above ingredients. Blend in mixing bowl until smooth. Grease a 10-inch iron skillet. Place skillet in oven. Bake 15 minutes at 400° until puffy and golden brown. Sprinkle with powdered sugar.

William Neacy

SAUERBRATEN

3 lbs. beef, round or shoulder
½ c. vinegar
½ c. water
1 small onion, thinly sliced
2 bay leaves
3 whole cloves
2 t. salt
  Dash of pepper
4 T. fat
1 c. water

Place beef in a bowl. Combine first 6 ingredients and blend. Pour over meat. Marinate 24 hours. Melt fat in a heavy skillet or Dutch oven. Add meat. Brown thoroughly. Add water to meat liquid and pour over meat. Cover. Simmer over low heat 3 hours or until meat is tender. Remove meat. Make gravy from juices in pan. Serves 6.

SAFFRON CAKE

1 c. mashed potatoes	½ c. shortening
	¼ t. saffron
½ c. sugar	¼ c. boiling water
1 pkg. granular yeast	2 eggs, well beaten
	1 c. sugar
1 c. potato water	½ t. salt
1 c. milk	8 c. bread flour

Thoroughly mix potato and ½ cup sugar. Dissolve the yeast in lukewarm potato water, add to potato and sugar mixture. Cover. Let set in a warm place about 3 hours. Pour boiling water on saffron. Bring milk to a boil, add shortening, eggs, sugar, salt. Carefully drain saffron water into this mixture (save saffron for crumbs). When lukewarm, add yeast mixture and 4 cups flour. Beat well. Cover. Let rise until bubbly, about 1 to 1½ hours. Add remaining flour or enough to make a dough that can be kneaded until smooth. Place in a greased bowl, cover and let raise about 4 hours or until double in bulk. Roll about ⅓-inch thick and place on greased cookie sheets or baking pans. Brush tops with butter, cream or beaten egg. Cover with crumb mixture. Let rise about 1 hour or until double in bulk. Bake at 325° for 20 to 25 minutes. Makes four 9-inch cakes.

CRUMBS

2 c. light brown sugar	1 t. cinnamon
2½ c. flour	1 c. shortening
	Saffron

Mix above ingredients well with hands. Crumbs must be richer than pie dough.

Mrs. Homer Kriebel

POUND CAKE

1 c. butter	3 c. flour
½ c. shortening	½ t. baking powder
3 c. sugar	1 c. milk
5 large eggs	2 t. vanilla

Mix butter, shortening, sugar and eggs together. Mix at least 20 minutes, until sugar is dissolved. Blend in flour and baking powder, then milk and vanilla. Mix well. Bake in greased bundt pan at 325° for approximately 45 minutes to 1 hour or until a toothpick inserted in center comes out clean.

Mrs. Charles Karlik

LEBKUCHEN

4 c. white syrup	3 T. cinnamon
4 eggs	1 c. water
4 c. sugar	1 T. anise seed
1 lb. citron	1 T. fennel seed
1 lb. almonds	1 T. cloves
9 T. vinegar	3 T. baking soda
2 T. ginger	Almond halves
1 T. salt	

Put citron, nuts and seeds through a food chopper. Mix all ingredients together except water and soda. When thoroughly mixed add soda to water and stir into mixture. Add flour to make a stiff dough (about 11 cups). Roll out dough about ⅜-inch thick. Cut with a 2½-inch round cutter and put on a greased cookie sheet. Ice with the following frosting. Place half an almond on top of each cookie. Bake at 350° for 10 to 12 minutes.

ICING

To 4 slightly beaten eggs add 4 cups powdered sugar. Spread very thin.

Note: These cookies improve with age.

Mrs. Lloyd Wehrly

Expressing national characteristics in their food, German dishes are quite hearty. Favorite German menus include sweet and sour foods, marinated pot roasts and fruit and vegetable combinations.

LUCHER CREAM

1 c. tapioca
2 egg whites, stiffly beaten
2 oranges, cut in small pieces
Juice of 1 lemon
1 small can crushed pineapple, drained
2 c. sugar
1 pt. whipped cream, whipped

Soak tapioca in cold water overnight. In the morning place in a double boiler and cook until clear, adding more water if needed. Remove from heat, allow to cool, slightly beating it, then pour in the egg whites. Set aside.

Mix the oranges, lemon juice, pineapple and sugar. Add tapioca and egg mixture and set in a cool place to chill. When cold add whipped cream. Serves 20.

Craig E. Sathoff

HONEY CURLS
(DIPLES)

6 eggs	4 c. oil (for frying)
2¾ c. flour	1 t. vanilla
⅓ c. oil	

Beat eggs well with vanilla and add flour slowly, kneading lightly. Add ⅓ cup oil and mix well. Separate dough into five sections. Keep unused portion covered to keep from drying. Roll one part on floured board until paper-thin. With pastry wheel, cut in strips 2-inches wide and length of pastry. Roll on fork to form circle. Drop into very hot oil, so dough will rise properly. Drain on absorbent paper.

SYRUP

Boil 10 to 15 minutes: 2 cups honey, 1 cup water, 2 tablespoons sugar. Dip diples in hot syrup, sprinkle with cinnamon and nuts.

Note: Best results are obtained by using a deep fat fryer. Do not use a frying pan.

Frocene Adams

MOUSSAKA

1 lb. ground chuck
2 medium eggplants
2 medium onions, chopped
2 T. chopped parsley
1 c. water
½ c. tomato paste
2 eggs, well beaten
½ c. grated aged American cheese
¼ lb. butter
½ c. olive oil
½ c. bread crumbs
Salt and pepper to taste

Brown meat and onion in olive oil. Add water, tomato paste, parsley, butter and salt and pepper. Simmer until liquid is absorbed, about 1 hour.

Peel eggplants and cut lengthwise in ¼-inch-thick slices. Sprinkle with flour. Sauté in olive oil until well coated. Add 2 tablespoons bread crumbs to chopped meat, mix well. Butter a baking dish and sprinkle with bread crumbs. Place half of the eggplant slices in dish. Spread half of meat mixture alternately. Pour eggs on top. Spread evenly. Sprinkle with grated cheese and bread crumb mixture. Bake in a 350° oven about ½ hour or until golden brown.

Greece, a seafaring nation located in the Mediterranean, has Armenian, Turkish and Persian elements in its cooking, and incorporates such local foods as eggplant, tomatoes, olive oil and fish.

SPINACH PIE

2 lbs. spinach
1 lb. feta cheese
7 eggs, beaten
¾ c. olive oil
2 T. butter, melted
½ lb. pastry sheets
Salt and white pepper to taste

Chop spinach into a large mixing bowl. Add eggs to spinach. Break cheese into small pieces and mix with spinach. Mix butter with olive oil.

Grease a 9 x 13-inch pan and place 6 pastry sheets into pan, brushing each with the butter-oil mixture. Spread spinach mixture over pastry sheets and cover with 6 individually greased pastry sheets. Bake at 350° for 1 hour. Cut in squares. Serves 15.

PASTRY SHEETS

5 c. flour   ¼ c. olive oil
1 t. salt   1¼ c. lukewarm
1 egg   water

Sift flour and salt into a large mixing bowl. Make a well in the center. Place egg, oil and water in well and stir. Gradually mix flour with all ingredients and knead dough until smooth and elastic. Cover. Set aside for 1 hour to raise. Shape a piece of dough into a ball about the size of an orange and roll out on a floured board until paper–thin. Set each sheet aside and cover with heavy waxed paper until dough is used up. Makes 15 sheets.

LAMB OVER NOODLES

1½ lbs. boneless lamb, cubed
¼ c. canned tomato paste
1 envelope onion soup mix
2 c. water

In a Dutch oven or heavy saucepan heat a small amount of shortening; brown meat well. Stir in onion soup mix, tomato paste, water. Simmer, covered, 1½ hours or until meat is tender, adding more water if needed. Serve over noodles.

HOLLAND

KALE AND SAUSAGE

3 lbs. kale
3 lbs. potatoes, peeled and quartered
1 lb. smoked sausage
Milk, boiled
Salt and pepper to taste

Remove and discard stems from kale. Wash and chop the leaves very fine. Place in a large kettle, add boiling salted water to just about cover and boil about 40 minutes. Add potatoes and sausage and enough water to prevent burning. Cook 30 minutes. Remove sausage. Mash potatoes and kale and stir in enough milk to make a smooth consistency. Add seasoning to taste.

ENDIVE WITH SAUCE

8 endive, sliced   ½ c. milk
1 T. butter, melted   Dash of nutmeg
3 T. flour

Place endives in salted water and boil about 10 minutes, or until tender. Drain, set aside stock. Combine butter and flour. Stir in milk and enough stock to make a thick sauce. Add seasoning. Pour sauce over endives. Serve.

DUTCH PEA SOUP (ERWTENSOEP)

1 lb. split peas
1 medium pig hock (or a medium pork shoulder)
3 qts. water
Salt and pepper to taste
3 medium onions, cut fine
3 potatoes, peeled and diced
2 carrots, peeled and sliced or diced

Cook meat, peas and water together until peas are smooth and meat is tender. Add the next four ingredients and cook until carrots are done. Simmer until ready to serve if desired. (Leftover soup will need to be thinned with water.)

Eva Kobes

APPLE PANCAKES (APPELPANNEKOEKEN)

2 c. flour   1¾ c. milk
4 t. baking powder   ⅓ c. melted fat
1 t. salt   3 green apples
2 T. sugar   1 t. cinnamon
1 egg, well beaten   ½ c. brown sugar

Mix dry ingredients thoroughly. Combine egg, milk and fat. Add to dry ingredients and stir until combined. Batter will be lumpy. When ready to bake pancakes, peel and thinly slice apples. Pour about ⅓ cup batter for each pancake onto hot griddle, top with single layer of apple slices. When bubbles appear, turn and bake other side. Remove from griddle, drizzle on melted butter and sprinkle with a sugar and cinnamon mixture. Cover and keep warm until ready to serve.

TASTY COLE SLAW

½ head cabbage,   1 egg, beaten
  shredded   1 T. brown sugar
¼ c. vinegar   1 T. celery seed
1 t. salt

Combine cabbage, vinegar, salt in a deep saucepan. Cover. Steam over low heat until tender, about 15 minutes. Drain. Pour remaining ingredients over cabbage. Cover, let stand 5 minutes before serving.

FISH IN WINE SAUCE

1 onion, chopped
1/8 stick butter or margarine
1/2 c. sherry wine
3 or 4 fillets of sole
　Juice of 1/2 lemon, strained
　Flour

Brown onion in butter or margarine until onion is clear and tender. Add wine and lemon juice and cook until bubbly. Lower heat. Place floured fillets on top of sauce. Cover and simmer about 15 minutes, basting sauce over fillets.

Gladys Hilpertshauser

BEEF AND ONION STEW

2 large onions, thinly sliced
1/4 c. flour
1/4 c. butter or margarine
2 c. stock
3 bay leaves
5 cloves
1 T. vinegar
1/2 lb. sliced leftover meat
2 T. flour
　Pepper to taste
　Worcestershire sauce to taste

Brown the onions and the flour in butter. Add stock gradually, stirring constantly. Add bay leaves and cloves. Cover and simmer for 5 minutes. Add the vinegar and the leftover meat, simmer for 1 hour. Mix the flour with a little water. Add to the stew to thicken sauce. Simmer 5 minutes, stirring constantly. Season to taste.

A land of canals, windmills and wooden shoes, the Old World charm of Holland is expressed in its cuisine. Fish and seafood dominate the national diet, liberally enhanced with such spices as ginger, cinnamon and nutmeg.

DUTCH DOUGHNUTS
(OLIE BOLLEN)

2 eggs, well beaten
1 qt. scalded milk (cool to medium lukewarm)
2 cakes yeast
2 c. sugar
2 1/2 lbs. flour (or enough to make a drop batter)
1 t. salt
1 1/2 lbs. raisins

Dissolve yeast in lukewarm milk, add other ingredients and beat well. Let rise until double in bulk. Drop by tablespoons in 375° deep fat. Drain on absorbent paper. Place in bag with granulated sugar and shake. Add 1/2 pound fruit mix if desired.

Mrs. Kenneth E. Coon

SPICE CAKE
(ONTBIJTKOEK)

2 c. self-rising flour
1/2 c. brown sugar
1/3 c. molasses
1 c. milk
1 t. each: ground cloves, cinnamon and ginger
1/2 t. grated nutmeg
　Pinch of salt

Combine all the ingredients to a smooth paste. Butter an oblong 8 x 3-inch cake tin, fill with dough and bake for about 1 hour in a 300° oven. Allow to cool. Keep in a tin or in bread bin with the bread for 24 hours before serving.

STEAMED PUDDING
(JOHN IN THE POCKET)

1 cake compressed yeast
3 c. sifted flour
1 egg, well beaten
3/4 to 1 c. milk
1/3 c. raisins
1/3 c. currants
1/3 c. orange peel
　Salt to taste

Scald milk and cool to lukewarm. Dissolve yeast in the warm milk. Add egg and milk and yeast mixture to the flour. Dough will be sticky. Work in the raisins, currants, orange peel and salt. Cover and let rise in a warm place 45 minutes to 1 hour. Meanwhile sprinkle a clean wet cloth with some flour. Tie dough into cloth, place in boiling water and simmer 2 to 3 hours. Remove from cloth. To serve, slice pudding and spread with melted butter and brown sugar.

HUNGARY

COFFEE CAKE

1 c. lukewarm milk	1 cake yeast
¼ c. sugar	1 egg
1 t. salt	3½ c. flour
¼ c. soft shortening	

Mix together first 4 ingredients. Add yeast. Stir until yeast is dissolved. Stir in the egg. Mix with a spoon and then by hand, adding flour in two additions for easy handling.

Turn dough on a floured board and cover for 10 minutes. Knead until smooth. Make a mound and place in a greased bowl. Cover with a damp cloth and set in a warm place until double in bulk, about 2 hours. Punch down and let rise again until not quite double, about 45 minutes. Punch down and mound up on board 15 minutes.

Cut walnut-size pieces and form into balls. Roll in melted butter, then roll in a mixture of ¾ cup sugar, 1 teaspoon cinnamon and ½ cup chopped nuts. Place in layers in a greased tube pan. Add raisins if desired. Let rise again about 45 minutes. Bake at 375° for 35 to 40 minutes.

Mrs. Howard Davis

As the visitor to Hungary travels south and west, mountains give way to flat plains on both sides of the Danube. Hungarians prefer unusual dishes, spicy and hot, and goulash has become the widely accepted Hungarian dish.

PORK SAUSAGE LOAF

1 c. diced mushrooms
2 T. butter
1 egg, beaten
1 lb. fresh bulk pork sausage
2 c. dry bread crumbs
1 t. paprika

Melt butter in a skillet and add mushrooms. Sauté. Combine sausage, mushrooms, egg and crumbs and shape into a loaf. Sprinkle with paprika. Place in a small roaster. Cover. Bake at 350° for ½ hour. Uncover, return to oven and bake 30 more minutes. Serves 4.

NUT BREAD

4 c. flour
1 t. salt
½ c. sugar
½ c. butter, softened
1 t. vanilla
2 eggs
1 pkg. dry yeast
1 c. lukewarm
  water
  Milk
  Walnuts
  Raisins

Mix together first 6 ingredients. Dissolve yeast in lukewarm water. Add yeast and enough milk to make a stiff dough. Knead until smooth. Put in a warm place until double in bulk. Divide into 2 equal parts. Roll out flat to about 1½ inches thick on a lightly floured board. Sprinkle with finely chopped walnuts and white raisins with a little sugar. Roll up lightly. Pinch ends together. Brush top with evaporated milk. Bake in a 350° oven 45 minutes. Yield: 2 loaves.

HUNGARIAN CABBAGE

Using a kraut cutter, cut up four medium heads of cabbage into a granite dishpan or stone crock. Add enough salt so that the cabbage is salty but not briny. Add a tablespoon each of peppercorns, dill seed, bay leaf and caraway seed. Work cabbage with hands until the mixture becomes watery. Cover with a plate and weight. Every day for 3 or 4 days, stir kraut. Replace weight each time after stirring. Put in containers and freeze.

Ruby Davenport Kish

HUNGARIAN GOULASH

3 lbs. veal, cut in 1-inch cubes
3 large potatoes, diced
½ c. water
1 t. salt
3 large onions, sliced
½ t. paprika
1 c. butter
1 c. cream
½ t. black pepper

Heat butter in a saucepan until hot, add onions and sauté. Add veal and sauté with onions until brown. Add water and cover. Cook until meat is tender, then add seasonings and potatoes. Cover. Cook until potatoes are tender. Add cream. Cook 5 more minutes. Serves 6.

INDIA

CURRIED RICE

1 c. uncooked rice
2 c. chicken broth
1 T. butter or margarine
1 t. salt
½ to 1 t. curry

Combine all ingredients in a 3-quart sauce-pan. Bring to a boil, stirring once. Lower heat to simmer. Cover pan and cook 14 minutes (or follow package directions). Fluff rice lightly with a fork. Pack rice into 6 individual buttered custard cups. Invert onto serving platter with baked chicken. Makes 6 servings.

To bake rice, use the same amount of ingredients but use boiling chicken broth. Bake covered at 350° for 25 to 30 minutes (or follow package directions).

SNOW PEAS

½ lb. fresh snow peas
4 T. butter, melted
1 t. salt
½ c. water

Wash snow peas, remove the strings. Combine butter, salt and snow peas. Mix well. Then add water. Cook uncovered for about 12 minutes, until all the water has been absorbed. Serves 4.

FRIED CAKES

2 c. flour
1 t. cinnamon
1 c. sugar
1 c. milk
½ c. butter
1 cake compressed yeast
1 T. warm water
Butter or margarine

Sift flour and cinnamon together. Mix flour and milk to a smooth paste. Add the sugar and butter and cook, stirring constantly until thick and clear. Remove from heat. Cool to lukewarm. Dissolve yeast in warm water. Add yeast to mixture. Set aside until cold. Shape into balls and fry in butter or margarine.

CURRIED FRUIT BAKE

2 cans (1-lb. 13-oz.) cling peach halves
1 can (1-lb. 4-oz.) pineapple slices
1 can (1-lb. 13-oz.) pear halves
6 bottles cherries with stems
½ c. butter, melted
1 c. light brown sugar, packed
6 t. curry powder

Drain fruits, dry well on absorbent paper towels. Arrange in 2-quart baking dish. Add sugar and curry powder to the butter. Spoon over fruit. Bake uncovered 1 hour at 325°. Serves 20.

Mrs. G. A. Hoffman

Bounded by the Himalayas on the north, India is the seventh largest country in the world with diversified languages, customs and people. Curried food has practically become synonymous with Indian cuisine.

FAR EAST CHICKEN LIVERS

8 chicken livers
4 pieces onion, ½-inch thick
1 egg yolk
Salt and pepper to taste
Bread crumbs

On a skewer place 1 chicken liver, a piece of onion, 2 chicken livers, another piece of onion and another chicken liver. Repeat until used up. Dip into egg yolk, then season with salt and pepper. Roll thoroughly in bread crumbs. Broil 5 to 6 inches from heat at 450° for 12 to 15 minutes. Brown on all sides. Serves 2.

CUCUMBER RAITA

2 c. plain yogurt
1 cucumber, peeled and grated
¾ t. ground cumin
Salt and black pepper to taste
Cayenne pepper to taste
Chopped parsley or coriander leaves

Combine yogurt, cucumber, ½ teaspoon cumin, salt and black pepper to taste. Chill. Sprinkle with black pepper, cayenne pepper, ¼ teaspoon cumin and parsley.

CURRIED BEEF AND EGGPLANT KABOBS

2 lbs. beef sirloin tip, cut in 1½-inch cubes
1 c. apple juice
¼ c. salad oil
¼ c. lemon juice
¼ c. brown sugar
2 T. soy sauce
2 T. instant minced onion
2 T. curry powder
1½ t. salt
⅛ t. pepper
1 small eggplant
½ c. Thousand Island dressing
1 c. fine dry bread crumbs
   Pitted ripe olives

Combine apple juice, salad oil, lemon juice, brown sugar, soy sauce, onion, curry powder, salt and pepper. Simmer 5 minutes, stirring to blend. Cool. Pour over meat, turn to coat each piece, cover and let marinate in refrigerator 4 to 6 hours or overnight. Pare eggplant, cut in half lengthwise and then crosswise into slices ⅓- to ½-inch thick. Spread slices with dressing and roll in crumbs to coat evenly.

Place alternately on four 12-inch skewers: marinated cubes of beef, pieces of eggplant and pitted ripe olives. Broil 3 to 4 inches from heat, brushing with marinade and turning to brown all sides of meat. Broil to desired degree of doneness, 15 to 20 minutes. Serve on a bed of rice. Makes 6 to 8 servings.

GLAZED CORNED BEEF AND VEGETABLE PLATTER

4 to 6 lbs. corned beef brisket
1 T. whole mixed pickling spices
  Water
⅓ c. orange marmalade
2 T. brown sugar
2 t. prepared mustard
3 green pepper rings
8 small potatoes, pared
1 10-oz. pkg. baby Brussels sprouts
  (frozen in butter sauce that clings)
1 10-oz. pkg. honey-glazed crinkle cut
  carrots (frozen in cooking pouch)
¼ c. sliced green onions (including
  some green tops) ·
  Seasoned pepper

Place corned beef in a Dutch oven, sprinkle with spices and barely cover with water. Simmer 3 to 4 hours, until meat is tender. Remove meat, reserving liquid in pan, and place on a rack in open roasting pan. Combine marmalade, brown sugar and mustard in a small saucepan and heat to boiling, stirring frequently. Brush mixture over corned beef. Bake in a 350° oven for 20 minutes, brushing with glaze occasionally. Arrange green pepper rings on top of meat before applying final glaze.

Add potatoes to cooking liquid when corned beef is removed, bring to a boil and cook 20 minutes or until tender. Drain. Cook Brussels sprouts and carrots according to package directions. Pour contents of pouches into bowl and stir in potatoes, green onions and seasoned pepper. Arrange vegetables around corned beef on a serving platter.

SHRIMP CHOWDER

1 large onion, sliced
¼ pt. boiling water
3 medium potatoes, sliced
  Salt and pepper to taste
1 pt. shrimp
1 pt. milk
1 to 2 ozs. grated cheese
  Chopped parsley

Sauté onion in some hot butter or margarine until tender. Do not brown. Add boiling water, potatoes and salt and pepper to taste. Cover. Reduce heat and simmer for 15 minutes, or until potatoes are tender. Add shrimp and milk and bring to a boil. Stir in cheese and parsley. Serve immediately.

HORSERADISH MOLD

1 3-oz. pkg. lemon gelatin
1 c. boiling water
½ c. cream-style prepared horseradish
1 t. salt
1 t. grated lemon rind (optional)
1 c. heavy cream, whipped
4 drops green food coloring

Dissolve gelatin in boiling water. Stir in horseradish, salt and lemon rind. Chill until partially congealed. Fold in whipped cream and food coloring. Pour into lightly oiled 1-quart mold. Chill 4 hours or until firm. Yield: 8 to 12 servings.

Note: When served as a salad, decrease the horseradish to ¼ to ⅓ cup.

IRISH SODA BREAD

2 c. plain flour
1 t. (level) baking soda
¼ t. salt
½ c. buttermilk (or sour milk)

Mix dry ingredients. Add buttermilk and stir to a soft dough. Turn onto floured board. Knead lightly. Shape into flat round and cut into 4 sections. Bake on hot griddle on top of stove 10 to 15 minutes. Turn once.

Ellie Rice

POTATO BREAD

1 c. mashed potatoes (warm)
1 t. salt
2 T. butter or margarine
  Flour
  Milk

Mix the potatoes, salt and butter. Add enough flour and milk to make a stiff dough. Roll out on floured board to ¼-inch thickness. Cut in 8 pie-shaped pieces. Bake on hot griddle on top of stove until both sides brown. Turn once.

Ellie Rice

WHEATEN BANNOCK

1 c. wholemeal flour
½ c. plain flour
1 t. baking soda
1 t. salt
1 t. sugar
Buttermilk

Mix dry ingredients. Make a well in center. Add enough buttermilk to make firm dough. Turn out onto floured board. Turn over once and bake in loaf or round pan in a 350° oven for 45 minutes.

Ellie Rice

IRISH RAISIN BANNOCK

4 c. flour
4 t. baking powder
1 t. baking soda
1 t. salt
2 T. sugar
1 T. butter
1 c. raisins
1¼ c. buttermilk
1 egg, beaten

Sift flour, baking powder, soda, salt and sugar together. Rub in butter, add raisins. Make a well and add buttermilk and beaten egg. Spoon into a well-greased 8- or 9-inch round casserole. Bake at 375° for 30 minutes, then turn oven down to 350° and bake for an additional 15 minutes.

Margaret Joniec

SAINT CLEMENT'S CAKE

½ c. self-rising flour
4 T. margarine
4 eggs
½ c. sugar
2 T. lemon curd

Sift flour into a bowl. Melt margarine in a small pan. Set aside to cool. Whisk eggs and sugar until very pale and creamy. Fold in flour and melted margarine. Pour into an 8-inch greased (deep cake) pan. Bake at 350° for 30 minutes. Turn out on a rack. Cool. Cut cake into three layers. Sandwich with lemon curd.

ICING

1¼ c. powdered sugar
Juice of ½ lemon
Slices of orange and lemon
crystallized candies

Sift powdered sugar. Mix with lemon juice and a little water to make icing stiff enough to coat back of spoon. Pour over cake so that top and sides are coated (do not spread). Leave to set. Decorate top of cake with strips of orange and lemon candy slices.

Margaret Joniec

LEMON CURD

½ lb. butter or margarine
½ lb. sugar
4 eggs, slightly beaten
Juice of 2 or 3 lemons to taste

Melt sugar and butter in a double boiler. When warm stir in eggs and lemon juice. Continue to stir until mixture thickens. Remove from heat and store in a dry jar in the refrigerator.

Note: This makes a good spread instead of jam or jelly and a good filling for inside of cakes.

Margaret Joniec

SHAMROCK ROLLS

Prepare a basic roll dough. Shape the dough into small balls, brush with some butter, arrange 4 balls in each greased muffin tin cup. Bake according to directions on recipe.

IRELAND

Ireland, famous for the wearing of the green, is a land surrounded by the sea and thus fish is of prime importance. Ireland is also noted for its Irish stew, corned beef and cabbage and Irish coffee.

FRUIT SALAD TRIFLE

1 sponge cake
4 T. raspberry jam
1 15½-oz. can fruit salad
½ oz. chopped walnuts
6 to 10 wafer cookies
1 pt. custard
½ pt. thick cream
2 T. milk
   Glacé cherries
   Mint

Split cake in half. Place bottom half in glass bowl. Spread half of the jam over cake. Place top half in bowl. Spread remaining jam over cake. Strain juice from fruit salad and arrange on top of sponge cake. Sprinkle with 6 tablespoons of the juice. Place chopped walnuts and wafers on top. Pour hot custard over all and allow to cool. Whip the cream with the milk and spread over custard. Decorate with cherries and sprigs of mint.

WATERCRESS SALAD

4 c. watercress	½ t. celery seed
1 c. sour cream	Salt and pepper
1 T. vinegar	to taste

Cut away coarse stems from watercress. Place watercress in a bowl. Combine above ingredients. Add to cress.

IRISH STEW

⅓ c. flour
1½ t. salt
   Dash of pepper
1½ lbs. lean lamb, cut in 1-inch cubes
2 T. fat
3 c. water
3 medium onions, sliced
4 medium potatoes, cubed
1 turnip, diced
5 medium carrots, quartered
1½ c. frozen peas
¼ c. water

Combine flour, salt and pepper. Coat meat. Save remaining flour. Brown meat in hot fat in a 4-quart saucepan. Add water and cover. Simmer until meat is tender, about 1½ hours. Add onions, potatoes, turnip and carrots. Cover. Simmer 15 minutes. Add peas. Cover and simmer until vegetables are tender. Blend water with remaining flour. Add to stew. Stir. Cook until thick. Serves 6.

IRISH COFFEE

Heat a stemmed goblet or mug.

Pour in half of a glass of Irish whiskey.

Add 3 teaspoons of fine granulated sugar.

Fill goblet with strong black coffee to within 1 inch of the brim, stirring to dissolve sugar.

Add softly whipped cream, floating cream on top.

Note: Do not stir after adding cream, since the true flavor is obtained by drinking the hot coffee and Irish whiskey through the cream.

Loretta Hesterwerth

IRELAND

Irish mist—now Irish fog
Hangs heavy over field and bog.

It wets the woolly flocks that graze
And shrouds the lakes with mystic haze.

This veil from heaven which hides the view
Reveals a beauty fresh and new...

A fairyland not often shown
Where sure the leprechaun makes his home.

Ruth E. McCracken

CUCUMBERS IN SOUR CREAM

4 cucumbers, peeled
   Salt to taste
1 onion, finely chopped (optional)
1 c. sour cream
1 T. vinegar
3 T. sugar
   Pepper to taste

Cut cucumbers in thin slices. Place in a bowl and sprinkle with salt to taste. Add onion. Remove juices from cucumbers by pressing with a heavy plate. Drain. Combine remaining ingredients. Pour over cucumbers and blend thoroughly.

41

CHICKEN CACCIATORE

2½ lbs. frying chicken pieces
1 envelope seasoned coating mix for chicken (Italian flavor)
1 8-oz. can stewed tomatoes
1 8-oz. can tomato sauce
½ c. dry white wine
¼ t. rosemary leaves

Coat chicken with seasoned coating mix as directed on package, reserving any leftover crumbs remaining in shaker bag. Arrange chicken in single layer in a shallow baking dish. Bake at 400° for about 40 minutes, or until well browned. Meanwhile, combine stewed tomatoes, tomato sauce, wine, rosemary and reserved crumbs in a saucepan. Bring to a boil. Spoon sauce over part of each chicken piece in the pan. (Do not cover chicken pieces entirely.) Continue baking 10 to 15 minutes longer or until chicken is tender. Makes 4 servings.

Italy, bounded on three sides by the sea and on the north by the Alps, is famous for its tomato and pasta dishes, and the use of cheese, spices and garlic. Vegetables and salads are also important, and are served at lunch and dinner.

PORK CHOPS ITALIANO

4 pork chops, about 1-inch thick
1 t. salad oil
1 medium onion
½ clove garlic, sliced
2 large green peppers
2 8-oz. cans tomato sauce
½ bay leaf
1 T. lemon juice
⅛ t. dried sage
  Seasoned salt
  Pepper

Trim chops of excess fat, sprinkle with seasoned salt and pepper. In a large skillet, sauté chops until well browned, draining fat as it forms. Place chops in a 2½-quart casserole. Heat oven to 375°. Pour salad oil in a clean skillet. Sauté onions, garlic and green peppers until golden. Add tomato sauce, 1 teaspoon seasoned salt, ⅛ teaspoon pepper, bay leaf, lemon juice and sage. Simmer, covered, until vegetables are almost fork tender. Pour sauce over chops, covering thoroughly. Bake, covered, until pork chops are done, about 1 hour. Makes 4 servings.

Joan Glass

42

ITALY

ITALIAN SPAGHETTI

¼ c. butter, margarine or salad oil
1 c. chopped onion
2 cloves garlic, finely minced
1 c. mushrooms, chopped (optional)
1 lb. lean ground beef
½ c. chopped celery
3 T. flour
½ c. beef stock
¼ c. sour red wine
½ can tomato paste
2½ c. canned tomatoes
1 T. parsley
1 pkg. spaghetti
  Salt and pepper to taste
  Parmesan cheese (optional)

Melt butter in a heavy skillet or Dutch oven. Sauté onion and garlic 5 minutes. Add mushrooms and meat. Brown lightly. Add next 7 ingredients. Salt and pepper to taste. Mix thoroughly. Cover. Simmer approximately 30 to 40 minutes. Add more wine and beef stock if sauce gets too thick.

Put spaghetti in boiling salted water and cook until tender, about 10 to 12 minutes. Drain, rinse in hot water and drain again. Place on a warmed platter and top with meat sauce. Sprinkle with parmesan cheese if desired. Serves 4.

RISOTTO MILANESE

1 lb. rice
1 small onion, chopped
2 qts. chicken stock
½ c. mushrooms
¼ lb. butter
1 small box saffron
  Salt to taste
  Grated parmesan cheese

Sauté onion in butter, add mushrooms to browned onion and let simmer a few minutes. Add rice, stirring until butter is absorbed. Add broth gradually to keep rice moist. When broth has been absorbed, rice should be tender. Dissolve saffron in some warm stock and add to rice. Add salt to taste. Serve with grated parmesan cheese.

Marie De Ambroggi

ROUND STEAK ROMANA

1 beef round steak, cut ¾ to 1-inch thick
   (2 to 3 lbs.)
2 T. lard or drippings
1 1½-oz. pkg. spaghetti sauce mix
¼ c. flour
1 t. salt
⅛ t. pepper
1 8-oz. can tomato sauce
1¾ c. water

Cut round steak into 6 to 8 serving-size pieces. Brown meat on both sides in lard or drippings. Remove meat from pan and pour off drippings. Mix spaghetti sauce with flour, salt and pepper. Combine in skillet with tomato sauce and water. Heat, stirring constantly, until mixture comes to a boil. Reduce heat and add meat. Cover tightly and cook over low heat for 1½ to 2 hours or until tender. Turn pieces of steak once or twice during cooking. Serve with hot confetti shell macaroni. Makes 6 to 8 servings.

CONFETTI SHELL MACARONI

4 c. large-shell macaroni
1 T. salt
3 qt. boiling water
½ c. coarsely chopped green pepper
2 T. thin strips pimiento
2 T. butter
1 t. minced parsley (optional)

Add shell macaroni and salt to boiling water. Bring water to a boil again and cook macaroni for 8 minutes. Add green pepper and continue cooking for 3 minutes or until macaroni is just tender. Drain thoroughly. Stir in pimiento and butter. Turn into a serving dish and sprinkle with parsley if desired. Serve hot. Serves 6 to 8.

LASAGNA

1 lb. lasagna noodles, cooked
2 16-oz. jars meatless sauce
2 c. large curd cottage cheese
½ c. grated parmesan cheese
¾ c. chopped onion
1 lb. mozzarella cheese
1 clove garlic
3 t. salt
2 eggs, beaten
2 lbs. ground beef
1 t. Italian seasoning

Cook ground beef, garlic and onion in a large, heavy saucepan until beef is done. Add sauce, salt and seasoning and mix well. Simmer gently 15 minutes. Combine eggs and cottage cheese. Grease a 12 x 9½ x 2½-inch baking pan and arrange first layer of lasagna and then alternating layers of the remaining ingredients, ending with a top layer of sauce. Sprinkle with parmesan cheese. Bake at 350° for 50 minutes.

Julia K. Chapman

POTATO DUMPLINGS (GNOCCHI)

2 lbs. potatoes
1½ c. flour

Boil potatoes until tender, drain. Dry and mash. Mix well with flour to make manageable dough. Knead well and shape into finger-sized lengths. Press hollow into each roll and drop into rapidly boiling salted water. Boil about 8 to 10 minutes. Remove with slotted spoon and serve with a favorite tomato sauce.

Marie De Ambroggi

SAUTÉED ZUCCHINI

Cut zucchini in very thin slices. Sauté chopped onion, green pepper and fresh mushrooms (in amounts desired) in part olive oil and part margarine. Add zucchini and toss gently as it cooks, about 5 minutes. Zucchini should be slightly underdone. Add salt, pepper, Italian seasonings to taste.

VARIATION

Add leftover chopped meat roast, chopped celery or grated carrots.

Mildred Renda

ITALIAN PANETTONE BREAD

1¼ c. milk
1 c. shortening or butter
½ c. whiskey
1 t. almond extract
1 t. brandy extract
1 t. rum extract
1 t. anise extract
4 c. all-purpose flour
5 t. baking powder
1½ c. sugar
4 large eggs
½ c. pine nuts
½ c. currants
1 c. glacéd fruit, chopped

Grease and lightly flour the bottoms of two 8½ x 4½ x 2½-inch loaf pans. Set aside.

Heat until melted ¾ cup milk and the shortening or butter. Add ½ cup cold milk and stir. Cool to lukewarm. Mix together and add: whiskey and almond, brandy, rum and anise extracts. Sift together the flour, baking powder and sugar. Add to the above mixture and stir with a spoon. Beat in the eggs. Fold in nuts, currants and chopped fruit. Mix well. Turn into the two prepared loaf pans. Bake in a preheated 350° oven for 50 minutes or until done. Cool in pans.

Laura Pessagno

SICILIAN CHEESECAKE

1 sponge cake
1 lb. ricotta cheese
3 ozs. cream cheese
½ c. sugar
2 t. maraschino cherry juice
4 ozs. bitter chocolate, grated
2 t. glacéd fruit, chopped
½ c. vanilla sugar

Cut sponge cake into 3 layers. Beat cheeses together and rub through a fine sieve. Add sugar, chocolate, maraschino cherry juice and 1 teaspoon fruit. Mix well until creamy. Spread filling between layers. Decorate top with vanilla sugar and remaining fruit.

Vanilla sugar: Mix 1 teaspoon vanilla to ½ cup sugar.

Marie De Ambroggi

STEAK TERIYAKI

Broil steak to desired degree of doneness. Before removing from broiler baste both sides of steak with the following sauce. Turn over several times until a glaze forms. Remove and serve.

SAUCE

1 c. Japanese soy sauce
3 T. sugar
1 T. sweet wine
   Pinch of ginger (optional)

Heat soy sauce, then add sugar. Bring to a boil, mixing well. Remove from heat. Add wine and ginger. Mix well.

FRIED RICE

½ c. chopped mushrooms
6 green onions including tops, chopped
4 c. cooked rice
1 c. cooked diced chicken
½ c. chicken broth
2 t. Japanese soy sauce
   Salt (optional)

Sauté mushrooms and onions in a small amount of salad oil for a few minutes. Add rice and chicken and cook over medium heat, stirring constantly, for 3 to 4 minutes. Add broth, soy sauce and salt. Cook until liquid is absorbed and rice is hot.

RUMAKI

2 green onions
1 8-oz. can water chestnuts, drained
⅓ lb. chicken livers, washed, drained and halved
8 bacon slices, cut crosswise into halves
½ c. Japanese soy sauce
¼ t. ginger
¼ t. curry

Cut onion into 3-inch lengths. Fold a piece of liver around a water chestnut, wrap with a slice of bacon and a strip of onion. Fasten with a toothpick. Mix soy sauce, ginger and curry. Marinate livers about 1 hour, turning occasionally. Place on a rack in a shallow pan and bake in a preheated 400° oven until bacon is crisp, about 15 to 17 minutes.

SUKIYAKI

¾ c. water
2 T. oil
2 lbs. tenderloin or sirloin steak
3 bunches green onions, sliced
3 medium onions, quartered
3 carrots, sliced thin and parboiled
1 small can mushrooms
1 medium can bean sprouts
1 pkg. frozen spinach, thawed
   Japanese soy sauce to taste
   Cooked rice

To prepare sukiyaki, keep each type of food together in one section of pan while cooking.

Trim meat of fat and cut in paper-thin slices. In a skillet or 10-inch sukiyaki pan add meat one piece at a time to the water and oil. Push into corner of pan. Put onions in another corner of the pan. Add bean sprouts, mushrooms, carrots and spinach, keeping each separated. Add soy sauce to taste. Cook on medium heat 5 to 10 minutes. Do not overcook. Serve over rice.

Perfectionists in the art of preparing a meal, the Japanese cook seeks food to please the eye as well as the taste. Japanese cuisine has such basic items as rice, seafood, colorful vegetables and green tea. Unique flavorings give the food character.

SPINACH SALAD

1 lb. spinach
3 T. Japanese soy sauce
3 T. toasted sesame seeds
  Sesame oil

Wash spinach, leaving stems intact. Boil in water to cover, about 3 minutes. Press excess moisture from spinach. Chop spinach and divide into 4 servings. Sprinkle with soy sauce, sesame seeds and sesame oil to taste. Serve immediately in small individual bowls.

RED BEAN CAKE

2 lbs. red beans
2 ozs. unflavored gelatin
¼ c. water   4 c. sugar

Boil beans approximately three hours. Rub through a sieve. Dissolve gelatin in the water. Add the sugar and gelatin and cook slowly 6 to 8 hours. Turn into an 8- or 9-inch square pan. Cool. Cut into 1½-inch squares or rectangles. Wrap pieces in cherry leaves if desired. Serve with tea.

ORIENTAL PORK AND PEARS

2 lbs. boneless pork shoulder, cut in
  1-inch cubes
3 T. lard or drippings
1 t. salt
1 can (1-lb. 13-oz.) Bartlett pear halves,
  drained
¼ c. cornstarch
⅓ c. brown sugar
3 T. soy sauce
⅓ c. vinegar
1 medium green pepper, cut in strips
8 cherry tomatoes, cut in half
1 3-oz. can chow mein noodles

Brown pork cubes in lard or drippings. Cover. Cook over low heat 30 minutes. Pour off drippings. Season with salt. Reserve pear liquid and measure 1¼ cups syrup. Mix cornstarch and brown sugar. Stir in pear syrup, soy sauce and vinegar. Cook over low heat, stirring constantly, until thick and clear. Pour sauce over meat. Add green pepper strips and cook over low heat for 5 minutes. Remove seeds from tomatoes. Cut each pear in half lengthwise. Lightly fold tomatoes and pears into meat mixture and continue heating 1 minute, stirring several times. Serve with chow mein noodles. Makes 6 to 8 servings.

JAPANESE FRUITCAKE

4 eggs
1 c. butter or margarine
3 c. cake flour
2 c. sugar
2 t. baking powder
1 c. milk
1 t. vanilla
1 T. ground allspice
1 T. ground cinnamon
1 T. ground cloves
1 c. seeded dark raisins

Have eggs and butter at room temperature before using. In a bowl blend and mix eggs and butter until fluffy. Add one egg at a time. Then add sifted flour, sugar and baking powder to above mixture, alternating flour and milk. When blended, divide the entire batter in half. Add spices and raisins. Grease and flour four 8-inch round cake pans. Bake in a preheated 350° oven approximately 1 hour and 15 minutes or until done. Cake is done when it leaves the side of the pan or springs back when touched. Cool, then place on cake racks.

FILLING

3½ c. sugar
2 lemons, juice and grated rind
2 oranges, juice and grated rind
½ c. boiling water
1 coconut, grated
2 T. cornstarch

Bring first 4 ingredients to a boil. Add cornstarch mixed with enough water to dissolve. Cook until balls form when dropped in cold water. Add coconut. Spread between cake layers.

Pattie Price Pearson

PEAS AND RICE

½ c. butter or margarine, melted
½ c. sliced green onions
  (including green tops)
¼ c. minced parsley
1 10-oz. pkg. frozen peas
4 c. cooked rice (1½ c. uncooked)
2 t. grated lemon peel
2 T. Japanese soy sauce

In a skillet, sauté onions and parsley in the butter until limp, about 3 minutes. Add frozen peas to boiling salted water and bring to boiling point. Drain. Add rice, lemon peel, soy sauce and peas to the skillet. Stir over heat until heated through. Serves 4 to 6.

MEXICO

SOMBRERO BEEFSTEAK STRIPS

2 lbs. beef round steak, cut ¾-inch thick
3 T. cooking fat
1 8-oz. can tomato sauce
1 16-oz. can whole kernel corn, drained
1 small onion, thinly sliced
¼ c. water
2 t. chili powder
1 t. ground coriander
1 t. salt
1 medium green pepper,
**   cut in 1-inch pieces**
⅓ c. chili sauce
1 c. (4 ozs.) shredded Monterey Jack
**   cheese**

Slice steak in strips ⅛-inch thick and 3 to 4 inches in length. Brown strips in cooking fat; pour off drippings. Add tomato sauce, corn, onion, water, chili powder, coriander and salt. Mix thoroughly. Turn mixture into a shallow 2-quart casserole or baking dish. Cover tightly and cook in a 350° oven 45 minutes. Remove from oven. Stir in green pepper, top with chili sauce and sprinkle with shredded cheese. Cover. Continue baking 15 minutes. Serves 6 to 8.

Note: Partially freeze round steak so it can be cut easily into very thin strips.

> Three great mountain ranges divide Mexico, a country that rises from sea level to altitudes of over three miles. Beans and tamales are national favorites, while tortillas remain the most universal and basic of Mexican food.

MEXICAN BREAD
(TORTILLAS)

2 c. masa harina (cornmeal)
1⅓ c. warm water

Combine above ingredients to make a thick paste. Pinch off chunks and press flat in circles. Cook on a moderately hot, dry griddle, turning frequently until dry and lightly flecked with brown.

Doc Kingsley

HOT TAMALES

Corn shucks
Prepared chili
Masa harina (cornmeal)

Soak corn shucks in water. Make a thick paste of masa harina with juice of chili. Spread a thin layer of the paste over about a quarter of the corn shuck. Place about a tablespoon of the chili meat in the center of the paste. Roll up the corn shucks as for a cigarette. Fold the empty part of the shuck over the full part. Place the shucks in a pan with enough water to steam and cook for 1 hour.

Doc Kingsley

CHILI BEANS

1 qt. uncooked brown or chili beans
1 lb. hamburger
1 large onion, cut up
2 large cloves garlic, minced
2 t. chili powder
1 T. curry powder
1 qt. cooked tomatoes
1 piece suet (size of medium apple)
1 T. salt

Cook beans until about half done. Cut suet into small pieces and put into a skillet and melt. Add hamburger and fry until medium brown. Add onion and brown along with hamburger. Add tomatoes, chili powder, curry powder and the minced garlic to this mixture. Cook all together for a few minutes, then add to the beans and cook slowly for 2 hours. Add salt when beans are almost done. More meat or tomatoes may be used if desired. Slow, long cooking improves the flavor.

Mrs. Emil Gubler

MEXICAN WEDDING CAKES

1 c. butter	**2 t. vanilla**
4 T. sugar	**2 c. finely chopped**
2 c. flour	** pecans**

Cream butter and sugar, add flour, nuts and vanilla. Make into small balls and place on ungreased cookie sheets. Bake at 300° for 30 to 45 minutes. Remove from cookie sheets and roll in powdered sugar (or shake a few at a time in a sack of powdered sugar). When cool, roll or shake again in powdered sugar. Store in cool, dry place. Makes about 100 balls.

Iva Nethaway

BEEF OLÉ

2 to 2½ lbs. beef round steak,
  cut 1-inch thick
2 T. lard or drippings
2 medium onions, chopped
2 8-oz. cans tomato sauce
1 1¼-oz. pkg. taco seasoning
¼ t. hot sauce (optional)
¾ c. grated cheddar cheese
¼ c. crushed tortilla chips
1 avocado, peeled and cut in 8 wedges
1 medium tomato, cut in 8 wedges
6 pitted ripe olives, sliced
8 round slices lettuce, cut ¼-inch thick

Slice beef crosswise in thin strips approximately ¼-inch thick. Then cut in pieces 2 inches long. Brown beef strips in melted lard or drippings. Pour off drippings. Add onions, tomato sauce, taco seasoning and hot sauce. Stir over low heat to blend. Turn into a 9-inch round baking dish 2 inches deep. Cover and bake in a 350° oven for 25 minutes. Remove from oven. Sprinkle crushed tortilla chips and grated cheese on top. Arrange avocado and tomato wedges alternately in wheel fashion to top. Place olives in center. Return to oven and continue baking uncovered 10 minutes or until vegetables are heated through. Serve on round slices of lettuce. Serves 8.

OPEN-FACE SANDWICHES

1 lb. ground beef, chuck or round
1 c. coarsely chopped onion
1 T. shortening
1 T. flour
1½ t. chili powder
1½ t. oregano
1 t. salt
¼ t. cinnamon
3 to 4 dashes hot red pepper sauce
1 8¼-oz. can tomatoes
¼ c. chili sauce
¼ c. sliced ripe olives
8 to 10 tortillas or hamburger buns
1½ c. shredded cheddar cheese

Cook beef and onion in shortening until meat is gray in color and crumbly. Blend in flour and seasonings. Add tomatoes, chili sauce and olives. Mix. Cover. Cook slowly to thicken and blend flavors, about 20 minutes. Spoon about a third of the meat mixture onto crisp, hot tortillas or toasted hamburger buns. Top with cheese.

NORWAY

PICKLED BEETS

24 medium beets   3 c. white vinegar
1 c. sugar   2 bay leaves

Wash beets. Do not peel. Add water to cover and cook in boiling salted water until tender. Drain and cool. Peel beets and slice thin. Combine sugar, vinegar and bay leaves and bring to a boil. Pour over beets. Bring mixture to a boil and boil 1 minute. Place in sterilized jars and seal.

FRUIT SOUP

1 lb. fruit (prunes, dried apricots, dried peaches, dried pears)
3 apples, cored and diced
½ c. sugar
1½ qts. water
1 stick cinnamon
2 T. tapioca

Cook first 5 ingredients together until fruit is tender. Remove cinnamon and puree fruits in a blender. Return fruits to saucepan and add tapioca. Cook until clear. Serve warm or cold.

SARDINE PASTE

1 8-oz. pkg. cream cheese
½ t. salt
1 T. lemon juice
1½ t. garlic salt
¼ t. black pepper
2 3¾-oz. tins boneless and skinless sardines
1 T. chopped parsley
Dash hot pepper sauce
Capers for garnish
Parsley for garnish

Cream together first 5 ingredients. Drain and mash sardines. Beat into cheese mixture with parsley and pepper sauce. Form into a mound and garnish with capers and chopped parsley. Serve with toast fingers or thinly sliced bread.

MEAT-FILLED POTATO CAKES

6 c. cooled mashed potatoes   1 t. salt
1 egg   1 minced onion
1 c. flour   ½ lb. finely cubed pork

Mix first 4 ingredients together. Roll out on a floured board. Cut in cakes ½-inch thick. Brown meat and onion in hot fat in a skillet. Place mixture on half of the cakes. Cover with other half. Press edges together. Boil 2 quarts salted water and drop in cakes. Boil 10 to 12 minutes.

FISH PUDDING

2 lbs. haddock (or any white fish)
2 t. salt
⅛ t. pepper
Dash of nutmeg
2 T. cornstarch
2 pts. milk

Remove skin and all bones from fish and grind 7 times through a food chopper, using finest blade. Stir in seasoning and cornstarch gradually during the grinding. Stir the fish in a large bowl, gradually adding the milk. Place in a greased dish and steam over hot water 1 hour. Slice and serve with hot shrimp or lobster sauce. Serves 6.

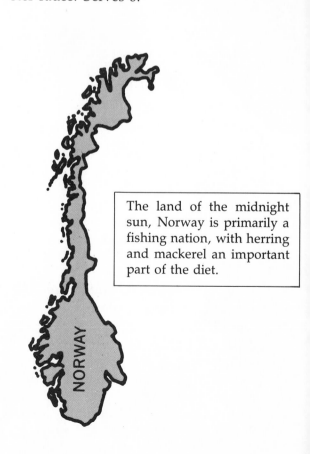

The land of the midnight sun, Norway is primarily a fishing nation, with herring and mackerel an important part of the diet.

KRUMKAKE

5 cardamom seed pods	1½ t. vanilla
	Dash of nutmeg
2 eggs, beaten	¼ c. butter
½ c. sugar	1 c. sifted flour
¼ c. heavy cream	

Crush cardamom seeds after removing from pods. Gradually add sugar to beaten eggs and beat until fluffy. Add cream, vanilla, cardamom, nutmeg and half of the butter. Beat until blended. Add flour and mix until smooth. Add remaining butter and mix. Place 1 level tablespoon of batter in center of preheated krumkake pan. Close lid and cook until lower side of cookie is light brown, about 3 minutes. Remove cookie from upper half of iron with a spatula. Roll while still hot around the handle of a wooden cooking spoon. Cool. Store in airtight metal containers. Serve plain or fill with whipped cream just before serving. Yield: 2 dozen cookies.

Note: Krumkake pans can be purchased in specialty hardware stores.

WAFFLES

3 c. flour   3 eggs
1 t. baking soda   1 c. sugar
4 c. sour milk   1 T. cardamom seed
2 T. melted butter Juice of 1 orange

Cream butter and sugar. Add eggs. Add a little of the flour and some of the milk. Dissolve soda in a cup of the sour milk. Add remaining ingredients. Place 1 tablespoon of batter in hot Norwegian waffle iron. Cook until golden brown.

Donna Kingsley

CHRISTMAS WASSAIL

1½ c. sugar   1 1-inch stick
4 c. boiling water   cinnamon
3 allspice   1⅓ c. orange juice
6 whole cloves   ⅔ c. lemon juice
1 T. ground ginger

Combine sugar and 2 cups of the boiling water and boil 5 minutes. Add spices, cover and set aside 1 hour. Add remaining water and fruit juices and mix well. Strain. Bring to a boil. Serve in bowl decorated with Christmas greens.

SAND BAKKELS

1 c. butter
½ c. brown sugar, firmly packed
½ c. powdered sugar
1 T. vanilla
1 egg
3 c. flour

Mix all ingredients together except flour until well blended. Gradually add flour to make a slightly soft dough. Press dough very thin into Sand Bakkel or tart tins. Bake at 400° for 10 minutes.

Evelyn Larson

NEVER-FAIL LEFSE

6 c. mashed potatoes 3 c. flour
2 t. salt   1 c. margarine
1 t. sugar

Mix together potatoes, sugar and salt and place in refrigerator overnight. Next day press potatoes through a ricer and set aside. Mix flour and margarine until dough is similar in consistency to piecrust dough. Combine flour mixture and potatoes. Form into small balls about 3 inches in diameter. Working with only 3 or 4 balls at a time, roll with a covered rolling pin or a specially ridged rolling pin. Bake dough on both sides on a lefse grill or pancake grill. To serve, cut dough into pie-shaped wedges, butter and roll up.

Mrs. Leonard Nelson

ROSETTES

2 eggs   ¾ t. vanilla
1¾ t. sugar   1 to 1¼ c. milk
¼ t. salt   1 c. sifted flour

Beat the eggs with the sugar and salt. Do not overbeat. Add flour, milk and vanilla alternately and blend until smooth. Beat lightly to break up as many lumps as possible. Heat deep fat until a bread cube browns in 1 minute (about 370°). Heat a rosette iron in the hot oil and dip the iron three-quarters of the way into the batter. Return the iron to the hot oil. Fry until lightly browned and drain on absorbent paper. When cool, dust rosettes with powdered sugar or dip them in granulated sugar while warm. Store in airtight containers. Makes 40.

HUNTERS' STEW
(BIGOS MYSLIWSKI)

This dish requires a minimum of last-minute effort. In fact, it must be prepared in advance, then reheated. Because it requires so many ingredients, it is seldom planned for less than a dozen people. The leftovers can be refrigerated, or may be cooked in large quantities and frozen for use later on, for the more Bigos is reheated, the better it tastes. The recipe asks for roast or braised meats plus its meat juices. If there is no time to roast or braise some of the meats before the dinner, meats can be cubed and slowly browned in fat and braised in a skillet and then used with all the drippings.

- 6 lbs. canned sauerkraut
- ¼ lb. bacon or salt pork, diced
- 3 large onions, chopped
- 3 tart apples, peeled and chopped
- 2 c. beef broth plus 1 c. sherry or dry red wine
  Salt, pepper, sugar to taste
- 3 to 4 lbs. roast or braised meats
- 1 bay leaf

Rinse the sauerkraut in cold water and squeeze out juice well, reserving some of the juice. Put sauerkraut in a large kettle over low heat. Meanwhile, render the bacon or salt pork. Add bacon bits to sauerkraut. Sauté onions in bacon fat until golden, add the chopped apples and cook until slightly browned. Add it all to kettle. Add the meats (diced) and all the meat juices. Add enough beef broth to simmer it all together. Add the bay leaf and salt, pepper, a little sugar and some of the sauerkraut juice for tartness. Simmer slowly for 1 to 1½ hours. Add the wine and let stew bubble up. Cover and let stand until ready to use.

Charlene Myers

POLAND

POLAND

ZUCCHINI FRITTERS

- 2 whole zucchini (or 1 cup, grated)
- 2 c. water
- 1 egg, beaten
- ½ t. salt
- ¼ t. garlic salt
  Pinch of baking soda
- 4 to 6 pumpkin blossoms, grated (optional)

Add to above ingredients enough flour to float the fritter on top of very hot vegetable oil in a skillet (2 tablespoons to each fritter). Smooth out to oval shape and brown. Serve while hot.

Mrs. Fonda Crislip

BEET SOUP

- 4 large beets
- 6 c. strong beef broth
- 1 onion, minced
- 1 t. sugar (or to taste)
  Salt and pepper to taste
- 2 T. lemon juice
- 3 T. minced dill
- 1 c. sour cream

Wash beets, peel and chop fine. Simmer in water to cover until tender, about 20 to 25 minutes. Simmer beef broth with onion for about 15 minutes. Through coarse sieve strain beef broth, discard onion. Then strain beet broth and strain about half the beets through sieve. Discard the rest. Combine the two broths. Season to taste with sugar, salt and pepper and lemon juice. Mix dill into sour cream and top each portion of hot soup with a spoonful of the sour cream-dill mixture, or use plain sour cream. Or serve chilled, with the sour cream-dill mixture stirred into it. Serves 6 to 8.

Charlene Myers

Surrounded by Russia to the east and Germany to the west, Poland's neighbors have had a strong influence on its food. Beet soup is an original Polish dish, although today it is considered a Russian specialty. Sauerkraut, noodles, dumplings and rich cakes are a result of the German influence.

SCONES

2 c. sifted flour	⅓ c. butter
3 t. baking powder	⅓ c. buttermilk
1 t. salt	1 egg
2 T. sugar	Sugar

Mix and sift dry ingredients. Cut in butter with a pastry blender. Add buttermilk to egg (reserve 1 tablespoon egg white). Beat until blended. Pour into dry ingredients all at once. Stir. Mix to moisten. Toss dough on a lightly floured bread board. Pat lightly and roll ¾-inch thick. Cut in squares or rounds with a floured knife. Beat remaining egg white with 1 teaspoon water. Brush each scone with mixture. Sprinkle with sugar. Bake on a cookie sheet in a 425° oven for 10 to 15 minutes, until golden brown.

SCOTCH MARMALADE

4 oranges	2½ qts. water
2 lemons	7 lbs. white sugar
2 grapefruit	

Boil fruit whole in the water for ½ hour. Cool and remove pulp. Put skins and all through a grinder, then measure back into the pot and add water to make 3 quarts.

Boil it all ¾ hour. Then add the sugar. Boil again for 15 minutes. Put in jars with wax on top.

Serve with shortbread, scones or oat cakes.

Edna Jaques

SCOTLAND

SCOTTISH SHORTBREAD

½ lb. butter	2½ c. sifted flour
½ c. sugar	Pinch of salt

Cream butter and sugar. Add flour and salt about a half a cup at a time. Mix well. Knead with hands if necessary. Press in ungreased 12 x 7½-inch pan. Make marks the length of the pan with tines of a fork. Bake in a 350° oven for 30 minutes or until light brown. Cut in 40 squares. If thicker squares are desired, bake in a 10 x 6½-inch pan for 45 minutes.

Maysie Newsom

Scotland, with rugged scenery and many natural resources, has several national dishes handed down from generation to generation. Much of the food is made with locally produced products . . . oats, barley, mutton, herring and haddock.

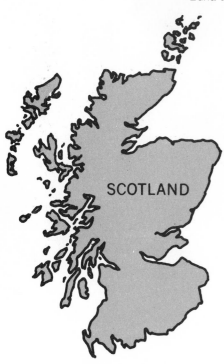

SCOTLAND

SCOTTISH COOKIES

1¾ c. sifted flour
¾ c. sugar
1 t. baking soda
½ t. salt
1 t. cinnamon
½ t. ginger
⅓ c. firm butter
1 c. oats, uncooked
½ c. dark corn syrup
2 eggs, beaten

Preheat oven to 350°. Mix and sift dry ingredients. Cut in butter until the size of peas. Add oats and mix. Combine syrup and eggs. Add to flour mixture and mix. Shape into balls, using 1 tablespoon of mixture for each ball. Place 2 inches apart on ungreased cookie sheets. Bake about 10 minutes. Yield: 4 dozen cookies.

LEMON TART

1 large cooking apple, peeled and grated
1 lemon
1 egg, beaten
¾ c. sugar
4 ozs. shortcrust pastry

Combine apple and sugar. Add grated rind and juice of lemon. Add egg to apple mixture, mixing well. Line a 7-inch tart plate with pastry. Add filling and bake in a 350° oven 25 to 30 minutes. Serve cold with cream or custard.

Nan McLean

HAGGIS

1 lb. steel-cut oats	1 onion
½ lb. minced suet	½ t. white pepper
¼ lb. liver	Salt to taste

Parboil liver, grate when cold. Mix all ingredients with water into a stiff paste. Tie in a pudding cloth three-quarters full. Put in boiling water and boil 3 hours.

Darlene Bartsch

SCANDINAVIAN POT ROAST

    3 to 4 lbs. beef arm or blade pot roast
    3 T. flour
1½ t. salt
  ⅛ t. pepper
  ½ t. ginger
    2 T. cooking fat
    1 cinnamon stick
  ½ c. water
    1 8-oz. pkg. mixed dried fruit
    1 c. orange juice
      Cornstarch (optional)

Combine flour, salt, pepper and ginger.
Dredge meat in seasoned flour. Brown pot
roast in cooking fat. Pour off drippings. Add
cinnamon stick and water. Arrange dried
fruit on pot roast. Cover tightly and cook
slowly 2½ to 3 hours or until meat is tender.
Add orange juice and cook slowly 15 minutes. Discard cinnamon stick. Remove meat
to heated platter. Thicken fruit and liquid
mixture with cornstarch for gravy if necessary. Makes 6 to 8 servings.

PANCAKES WITH LINGONBERRIES

1 c. sifted flour   3 c. milk
2 T. sugar   ⅓ c. butter
¼ t. salt   Lingonberry
3 eggs, beaten   preserves

Sift flour, sugar and salt together. Then add eggs and milk gradually. Stir until thoroughly mixed. Let stand 1 to 2 hours. Heat a griddle, skillet, or tempered Swedish pancake pan. Brush well with butter. Spread hot cake batter thin. Brown on each side. Roll hot cakes, serve with lingonberry preserves.

SWEDISH POTATOES

7 potatoes, peeled and diced
1 chopped onion
2 T. butter or margarine
1¾ c. milk
    Salt and white pepper to taste
    Chopped parsley (optional)

Brown the potatoes and onion in butter or margarine. Season. Add the milk gradually and simmer until potatoes are tender, about 15 minutes. Season to taste. Garnish with chopped parsley if desired. Serves 4.

SWEDISH MEATBALL STEW

1 2⅜-oz. pkg. Swedish meatball
    seasoning and sauce mix
⅓ c. water
1 lb. ground round or lean ground beef
2 T. butter or margarine
4 c. water
4 small onions, peeled
4 small potatoes, peeled
4 small carrots, scraped and cut
    into chunks
    Salt and pepper to taste

Blend seasoning mix with the ⅓ cup of water. Set aside for 5 minutes. Add meat, stirring well. Form into 12 meatballs and brown in sizzling butter for about 8 minutes, turning once. Place sauce mix in a large stewing kettle and slowly add the 4 cups of water. Mix thoroughly. Add meatballs and vegetables, then salt and pepper to taste. Cover. Simmer for approximately 1½ hours or until vegetables are fork tender. Serves 4.

Jacqueline Shafer

SWEDEN

SWEDISH COFFEE CAKE

1 c. boiling water   1 c. flour
½ c. soft butter   4 eggs
½ t. salt   1 t. vanilla

Bring water, butter and salt to boiling point. Remove from heat. Immediately add all of the flour, stirring vigorously until a smooth ball is formed that leaves side of pan. Add eggs one at a time, mixing well after each addition. Add vanilla and mix well. Cover. Let stand while making the following mixture:

½ c. butter
1 c. flour
1 T. water

Cut butter into flour until fine as meal. Sprinkle water on mixture and mix. Shape in roll about 28 inches long and arrange as a figure 8 on an ungreased cookie sheet. Flatten roll to a 4-inch width. Spread cooked mixture over entire surface. Bake at 425° about 25 minutes. Turn off heat and dry in oven about 10 minutes. Frost with a powdered sugar frosting.

Mrs. R. C. Sauer

Swedish food is famed primarily for the sumptuous smörgasbord, a table laden with from six to sixty various hors d'ouevres. But Sweden has other favorites as well . . . meatballs, pancakes with lingonberries and spicy desserts.

GINGER COOKIES
(PEPPARKAKOR)

1 c. white sugar   1 t. cinnamon
1 c. melted butter   1 t. baking soda
½ t. salt   ½ c. boiling water
1 c. dark molasses   1 egg
½ t. each ginger   3 c. flour
    and cloves

Dissolve baking soda in the boiling water. Mix all ingredients together. Roll thin. Cut dough with a cookie cutter. Bake at 325° until light brown. Watch carefully, as cookies brown very quickly.

Mrs. Edward J. Malec

SWITZERLAND

SWISS STEAK

⅓ c. flour
1 t. salt
 Pepper to taste
2 lbs. round steak, sliced thin
½ clove garlic
3 T. drippings
¼ c. chopped onions
2 c. canned tomatoes
½ t. paprika

Combine flour, salt and pepper, pounding it into steak with the blunt side of a knife. Cut steak into serving pieces. Brown meat on both sides in drippings in a skillet. Add remaining ingredients and heat to boiling. Reduce heat and cook, covered, until tender, about 1½ to 2 hours.

ALPINE LAND

Up, up, up they stand, the mountain
 thrones thrust high,
Where glaciers shine in the sun and
 ridges rub the sky.

Forests fade away . . . The tree becomes
 a vine
That crawls along rocky shelves above
 the timberline.

To alpine land, wild land, the special
 task is given
To lift man's spirit upward and tie the
 earth to heaven.

Robert B. Ward

GRAVY SOUP
(GERÖSTETE MEHLSUPPE)

5 T. butter, melted   5 T. flour
                         7 c. stock

Add the flour to the melted butter. Fry over low heat until deep brown. Add stock. Mix well. Boil at least 1 hour. Season to taste. Add croutons and grated Swiss cheese before serving.

PEAR BREAD

2 c. scalded milk   1 c. lukewarm water
3 c. sugar   3 lbs. raisins
4 t. salt   2 lbs. dried pears
1 c. fat   2 lbs. currants
2 c. water   1 to 2 T. anise powder
3 cakes   2 t. cinnamon
 compressed   Flour
 yeast

Combine scalded milk, sugar, salt, fat and water. Cool to lukewarm. Soften yeast in the lukewarm water. Stir in the yeast and enough flour to make a sponge dough. Add the fruit and enough flour to make a dough that will not stick to the board. Put into a bowl and let rise until double. Shape into loaves and let rise again until double. Bake at 225° about 2 hours.

CHEESE PIE
(KÄSE WAKE)

1 9-inch unbaked piecrust
½ lb. Swiss cheese, grated
1 T. flour
3 eggs, well beaten
1 c. milk
 Salt and pepper to taste

Combine cheese and flour. Spread in piecrust. Combine milk and eggs, add salt and pepper and pour over cheese. Bake at 400° for 15 minutes. Reduce heat to 325° and bake 30 more minutes or until a knife inserted in center comes out clean. Serves 6.

SWITZERLAND

Switzerland, a land of snow and beautiful scenery, is known for its chocolate and its cheese dishes. The national dish is cheese fondue.

SWISS FONDUE

- 1 lb. Swiss cheese, shredded
- 3 T. cornstarch
- ½ t. salt
- ¼ t. white pepper
- ¼ t. nutmeg or paprika
- 2 c. buttermilk
- 1 clove garlic
- 1 loaf French or Italian bread, cut in chunks with crust on each

Mix cheese with cornstarch, salt, pepper and nutmeg. In a chafing dish heat buttermilk with garlic clove over low heat. When hot, remove garlic and add cheese. Stir constantly until cheese is melted. Serve from chafing dish. Each person serves himself from the common dish, dipping chunks of bread speared on long forks into cheese sauce.

UNITED STATES

GROUND BEEF BARBECUE

1 lb. lean ground beef
1 chopped onion
1 chopped green pepper
1 T. sugar
1 T. vinegar
2 T. mustard
¾ c. catsup
   Salt and pepper to taste

Brown beef. Add remaining ingredients and simmer 30 minutes. Serves 8 to 10.

Mrs. Lois Pilyer

ALL-AMERICAN SALAD

½ c. crumbled American blue cheese
¼ c. milk
2 T. lemon juice
   Dash of Worcestershire sauce
½ head lettuce, broken in coarse pieces
½ c. diced celery
2 tomatoes, peeled and quartered
2 green onions, sliced fine
2 hard-cooked eggs, quartered
2 slices boiled ham, cut in strips
½ t. celery seed

Blend cheese, milk, lemon juice and Worcestershire sauce in bottom of a salad bowl. Add lettuce, celery, tomatoes and onions, mixing lightly until vegetables are coated with dressing. Arrange eggs and ham strips on salad and top with additional crumbled cheese and celery seed. Serves 4.

BASIC MEAT LOAF

1 egg
3 slices soft bread, torn in tiny pieces
1 t. salt
1½ lbs. ground beef
½ c. tomato sauce or catsup
1 t. onion salt

Preheat oven to 350°. Break egg into bowl, beat with fork. Add remaining ingredients and mix well. Place mixture into loaf pan. Pat evenly to make a smooth top. Bake for 1 hour.

Brenda Crosser

COUNTRY FRIED CHICKEN

1½- to 3-lb. frying chicken, cut in
   serving pieces
   Salt and pepper to taste
   Fat or oil
   Flour

Season chicken with salt and pepper. Roll in flour. In a heavy skillet, heat ¼ to ¾ cup fat or oil, enough to cover bottom of pan. Brown chicken pieces on each side. Continue to cook slowly, uncovered, until tender. Or cook in oven at 350° about 30 to 45 minutes, or until tender.

CORN CHOWDER

2 medium potatoes, peeled and diced
1 c. water
1 16½-oz. can cream-style corn
1 pt. milk
1 T. butter
   Salt and pepper to taste

Boil potatoes in water until thick. Add remaining ingredients. Heat and serve.

June Kissinger

> The cuisine of the United States is divided into localities—Midwest, South, East and Southwest. Corn dishes are most popular in the Midwest, seafoods in the South, chowders in the East and barbecued meats in the Southwest.

BAKED BEANS

4 cans (1-lb. 5-oz.) pork and beans
½ lb. bacon
1 c. chopped onion
½ c. light molasses
½ c. catsup
1 t. dry mustard

Preheat oven to 400°. Turn beans into a 3-quart casserole or bean pot. In a skillet, sauté bacon and onion until onion is golden. Remove from heat. Add molasses, catsup and mustard. Mix well. Gently stir into beans.

Bake, uncovered, 1 hour or until beans are hot and bubbly.

Mrs. Junior De Jonge

GRANDMOTHER'S ICE CREAM

1 can sweetened condensed milk
10 c. milk
2 T. flour
2 T. cornstarch
6 eggs, well beaten
1½ c. granulated sugar
1 c. brown sugar (packed)
3 T. vanilla

Heat 9 cups milk in a double boiler. Combine the flour, cornstarch, eggs, sugar and the remaining cup of milk. Add to the 9 cups of milk. Stir constantly. Cook until mixture coats a spoon. Strain through tea strainer. Cool. Just before freezing add flavoring and condensed milk. Freeze in ice cream freezer.

Mary A. Robinson

AMERICAN FAVORITE

American as corn on the cob,
Perennial as a picket fence,
As right as rain, when dust is deep,
And down to earth as common sense,
A freshly baked apple pie exudes
Enticing flavors from each slice,
Whose flaky crust and luscious fruit
Fling tantalizing whiffs of spice.
Parfait, cake, pudding or meringue
Cannot compete with juicy wedges
Of crisp brown pastry, flaunting frills
Of apple goodness on the edges.

Gail Brook Burket

APPLE PIE

Pastry for 2-crust 8-inch pie
5 c. pared, sliced tart apples
⅔ c. sugar
1 T. cornstarch
½ t. cinnamon
1 or 2 T. butter or margarine (optional)

Prepare unbaked pastry. Mix dry ingredients lightly with apples. Put filling into pastry-lined pan. Dot with butter if desired. Top with second crust. Bake at 400° for 40 to 60 minutes, or until filling bubbles and the crust is golden brown.

Note: If fruit is sweet, decrease amount of sugar, if unusually tart, increase sugar.

BROWNIES

¾ c. all-purpose flour
½ t. baking powder
¼ t. salt
2 eggs
1 c. sugar
½ c. butter or shortening
2 squares (2 ozs.) unsweetened chocolate
¾ c. chopped nuts
1 t. vanilla

Sift flour, measure and resift 3 times with baking powder and salt. Beat eggs until light and fluffy. Add sugar in 3 portions, beating well after each addition. Add butter and chocolate melted together in the top of a double boiler over hot (not boiling) water. Mix thoroughly, add flour mixture, nuts and vanilla. Beat only enough to blend well. Spread in a lightly greased 11 x 7 x 1½-inch or 8-inch-square shallow pan. Bake at 350° for 20 minutes. Do not overbake. Leave in the pan, cool slightly on cake rack, then cut in squares or oblongs while warm. Makes about 16 squares.

Judith L. Moudy

RICE PUDDING

2 c. milk	⅓ c. sugar
1 c. cooked rice	¼ t. salt
1 T. butter or margarine	⅓ c. raisins
	2 eggs, beaten

Heat milk. Add rice and butter. Add sugar, salt and raisins to eggs. Slowly stir in the hot milk mixture. Pour into a greased baking dish and set in a pan of hot water. Bake at 350° for 1 hour or until set.

MOIST CHOCOLATE CAKE

2 c. flour	1 c. oil
1 t. salt	1 c. hot coffee
1 t. baking powder	1 c. milk
2 t. baking soda	2 eggs
¾ c. cocoa	1 t. vanilla
2 c. sugar	

Mix all dry ingredients together. Add liquids. Mix at medium speed of electric mixer. Add eggs and vanilla. Bake in a 13 x 9 x 2-inch pan at 350° for 30 minutes.

Mrs. Robert G. Keely

61

YUGOSLAVIAN CHICKEN PAPRIKA

1 chicken, cut up
1 large onion
¼ t. chopped garlic
3 T. sweet paprika
1 c. water or chicken broth
1 c. sour cream
2 T. flour
Chopped dill or peppercorns (optional)
½ c. sweet cream

Salt chicken, then dip in flour. Brown until golden. Remove chicken from pan and add onion and garlic. Brown. Remove from heat and add paprika and water. Add chicken. Simmer 1 hour until done. Combine sour cream and sweet cream with flour and stir until smooth. Pour into pan, stirring constantly. Serve over hot biscuits or dumplings.

DUMPLINGS

1⅓ c. sifted flour
2½ t. baking powder
¾ t. salt
1 egg, well beaten
½ c. milk

Blend above ingredients. Drop with spoon into above chicken mixture. Simmer 15 to 20 minutes covered.

Mrs. C. J. Hogan

LEBANESE HOMMOS

2 c. chick peas
½ t. baking soda
2 cloves garlic, minced
¼ c. sesame or salad oil
1½ T. lemon juice
Toasted bread or crackers

Wash chick peas thoroughly and soak in water for 24 hours. Add baking soda to chick peas and cook in water in which they soaked. Cook until soft, about 1½ hours. Drain well. Place chick peas in bowl and chop fine, adding the garlic. Continue chopping while slowly adding the oil. Sprinkle lemon juice over chopped mixture. Serve cold with toast or crackers.

Edith Pikelny

MISCELLANEOUS

SOUTH AMERICAN SPICY CORN PUDDING

1 c. buttermilk
1 c. yellow cornmeal
1 c. sifted flour
3 t. sugar
1 t. salt
1 t. baking powder
½ t. baking soda
1 egg, beaten
¼ c. melted shortening
1 8-oz. can whole kernel corn, drained
½ 4-oz. can diced green ortega chilies
1 4-oz. can pimientos, drained and chopped
2 c. grated cheddar cheese

Combine milk and cornmeal. Let stand 30 minutes. Preheat oven to 375°. Grease a 9 x 13-inch pan. Sift dry ingredients, add egg, shortening and buttermilk mixture and stir well. Add corn, peppers and pimientos and stir well. Fold in cheese. Turn into pan and bake 30 minutes. Serve warm with butter as an accompaniment with meat.

Charlene Myers

NIGERIAN BEEF AND SAUSAGE

2 lbs. round steak, cut ½-inch thick
½ lb. smoked Thüringer, sliced in ½-inch diagonal pieces
¼ c. flour
2 t. salt
⅛ t. mace
2 T. lard or drippings
2 15-oz. cans black-eyed peas
1 16-oz. can tomatoes
2 medium onions, quartered

Cut round steak in strips ½-inch wide and 2½ inches long. Combine flour, salt and mace. Dredge strips in seasoned flour. Brown beef strips in lard or drippings. Pour off drippings. Drain black-eyed peas and add ½ cup of the liquid to the beef strips. Cover and cook over low heat 1 hour. Add sausage, drained black-eyed peas, tomatoes and onions, and continue cooking 30 minutes or until meat and vegetables are done. Thicken liquid with flour for gravy if desired. Serves 8.

INDEX